T0305755

FINANCIAL
MANAGEMENT
<small>and</small> CORPORATE
GOVERNANCE

FINANCIAL MANAGEMENT
and CORPORATE GOVERNANCE

Daisuke Asaoka
Meiji University, Japan & Kyoto University, Japan

World Scientific

EW JERSEY · LONDON · SINGAPORE · BEIJING · SHANGHAI · HONG KONG · TAIPEI · CHENNAI · TOKYO

Published by

World Scientific Publishing Co. Pte. Ltd.

5 Toh Tuck Link, Singapore 596224

USA office: 27 Warren Street, Suite 401-402, Hackensack, NJ 07601

UK office: 57 Shelton Street, Covent Garden, London WC2H 9HE

Library of Congress Cataloging-in-Publication Data
Names: Asaoka, Daisuke, author.
Title: Financial management and corporate governance /
   Daisuke Asaoka, Meiji University, Japan & Kyoto University, Japan.
Description: Hackensack, NJ : World Scientific, [2022] |
   Includes bibliographical references and index.
Identifiers: LCCN 2022002756 | ISBN 9789811252396 (hardcover) |
   ISBN 9789811254208 (ebook) | ISBN 9789811254215 (ebook other)
Subjects: LCSH: Management--Finance. | Consolidation and merger of corporations--Finance. |
   Investments--Management. | Corporate governance--Moral and ethical aspects.
Classification: LCC HG173 .A8143 2022 | DDC 658.15--dc23/eng/20220120
LC record available at https://lccn.loc.gov/2022002756

British Library Cataloguing-in-Publication Data
A catalogue record for this book is available from the British Library.

For any available supplementary material, please visit
https://www.worldscientific.com/worldscibooks/10.1142/12726#t=suppl

Desk Editors: Soundararajan Raghuraman/Pui Yee Lum

Typeset by Stallion Press
Email: enquiries@stallionpress.com

Printed in Singapore

About the Author

Daisuke Asaoka is an associate professor at Meiji University and an adjunct associate professor of finance at Kyoto University's Graduate School of Management. He earned an MBA from the University of California at Berkeley, graduating in the top 5 percent of his class, and an LL.B. and Ph.D. from the University of Tokyo. He is the author of *Corporate Finance: A Valuation Approach* (2006) and *Institutional Evolution and the Growth of Firms* (2012), both from NTT Publishing, *Corporate Finance* (2022) from Nikkei (co-authored), and *Corporate Architecture* (2022) from University of Tokyo Press.

Acknowledgment

I would like to thank Ms. Lum Pui Yee, the editor at World Scientific who invited me to write this book. Part of my work was supported by research grant JSPS (JP19K13811, JP21K01640). Special thanks go to my family, who give me inspiration and joy in every aspect of my life. I dedicate this book to them.

Contents

List of Figures

List of Tables

Introduction

The job of managers and entrepreneurs is to navigate their firms toward growth and financial viability. Each day they make decisions while dealing with uncertainty, competition, and threats in the markets. Achieving these goals in the face of such challenges requires a wide range of knowledge and skills. In examining key issues and aspects of financial management and the corporate governance architecture which underlies them, this book provides a basis for a solid understanding of firms, laws, and markets.

To start, it will be helpful to lay out the fundamental issues which concern firms as a whole. This will enable us to clarify the scope of this book by distinguishing what is dealt with here and what is not. Most importantly, this book is about *financial* management as opposed to general management. It also deals with corporate governance, which is intertwined with the management of firms. Finally, it is about firms as opposed to individuals.

1. What Is the Difference Between Management and Financial Management?

This book focuses on financial management by firms. Firms are involved in a number of parallel activities, such as strategic planning, research and development, sales and marketing, information and data processing, organizational design and behavior, and legal affairs and compliance, each requiring due care. Since such broad requirements exceed the scope of one individual's attention and time, firms are run by teams having different types of expertise and experience. Financial management, in which a firm's representatives interact with capital investors and increase corporate value in the financial markets, is one of these aspects. Since value is a lens through which financial managers look at firms and markets, their perspectives involve dealing with a fair amount of quantitative information and its economic interpretation.

Given that value is a financial expression of a firm's activities, financial managers grasp the underlying facts that drive value through its lens. Since most corporate activities ultimately relate to value, understanding such connections enables them, in turn, to provide key insights and inputs for their firm's survival and growth. Such insights can be diverse. They can include traditional ones involving strategy, operations, and information, as well as nascent ones on environmental, social, and governance issues. Firms today are facing increasingly complex and unpredictable circumstances, and managers must deal with changing realities. For this reason, this book provides essential frameworks for the financial management of firms. We make no claim that financial perspectives will solve all managerial problems, as if by a wave of a magic wand. But they do serve as a reliable compass for firms seeking to orient themselves during uncertain times.

2. What Is the Difference Between Corporate Management and Corporate Governance?

Corporate governance is an increasingly indispensable aspect of a firm's operation. Properly structured corporate governance architecture is a precondition for which managers are responsible. The need for governance arises from the various conflicts existing between the managers of firms and other entities, most prominently shareholders, with which they are involved. Firms are managed and governed simultaneously. Typically, management guides a firm's actions, while governance observes them. The latter act is often referred to as monitoring, implying a narrower, more passive scope of activities than management. But this is not always the case, as governance sometimes requires the proactive gathering of information and proposing of actions, rather than merely approving and seeing through actions proposed by management.

This dual layer of management and governance originates from the legal concept of a trustee. Since firms do business by obtaining external resources such as financial capital, the investors that provide that capital want someone other than a firm's managers to ensure that it is properly used, even if this adds to the overall cost of operations. If ownership is concentrated, this may be done by the investors themselves. Under a dispersed ownership, however, it is less costly vis-à-vis benefits if someone chosen by investors undertakes the role on their behalf, forming a trust relationship. This is usually a relationship in which someone — a trustee — takes care of an asset, or trust, for someone else — a beneficiary — with the trustee owing a fiduciary duty to the beneficiary. In this context, governance refers to the board of directors taking charge of capital provided by investors. This is a separate concept to management, which is primarily concerned with what firms do with the capital.

Although the functioning of a trustee is normally limited to assets such as securities and real estate, the concept is a common one in the figurative sense as well ("The Youth of a Nation are the trustees of Posterity."[1]). The prevalence of the dual layer indicates that people value such a mechanism for its role in ensuring that a firm's architecture is reliable and trustworthy enough for investors to feel secure in supplying it with capital.

3. What Is the Difference Between Individuals and Firms?

A firm is a legal construct called a corporation, established by corporate law. In this book, we use the terms *firm* and *corporation* synonymously in general, but we use the latter when emphasizing the entity's legal aspects. A firm, or corporation, is in a sense an abstract construct because unlike human beings, it does not have physical substance *per se*, and merely traces its legitimacy to a legal registry. There are a number of factors that give it substance: the people that work for it, for example, as well as office buildings, brands, websites, and the goods and services that result from its activities. Among these, an indispensable factor is its people, since corporate laws usually require that a natural person serves on boards of directors across jurisdictions. This means that a firm's decision is ultimately a human decision.

---

[1]Disraeli, B. (1845). *Sybil, or the Two Nations*. London, UK: Henry Colburn.

Although a business may be run by a single person, as may be the case with a shopkeeper, a freelance programmer, or an artisan, this book primarily looks at firms, such as large enterprises with multiple employees and the startups that grow into them, as opposed to sole proprietorships run by individuals. The implication is that these firms involve a number of shareholders and stakeholders in the course of doing business. In the financial markets, firms deal with investors, such as debtholders and shareholders, to finance their operations. This immediately gives rise to possible conflicts among managers, debtholders, and shareholders that require a governance mechanism to coordinate and protect each interest. Adding to the complexities of this relationship, firms also deal with a multiplicity of stakeholders, including employees, customers, suppliers, and the global and local communities in which they operate. Sole proprietorships have similar issues, since they too are part of this complex web of business networks involving a number of relationships, but the issues are more salient in larger firms.

4. Organization of This Book

Based on the perspectives behind these distinctions, this book is composed as follows. Chapters 1 and 2 lay out the fundamental concepts of financial management and the core topics of corporate finance. Chapters 3 through 5 deal with advanced topics in these fields, ranging from asymmetric information and capital structure to mergers and acquisitions. These chapters look at financial transactions and decisions involving conflicts that call for a governance perspective, such as those between managers and investors, debtholders and shareholders, and sellers and buyers. Chapter 6 deals with the topic of stakeholder value, which adds further layers of perspectives on firms. Finally, Chapter 7 discusses corporate governance with an emphasis on comparisons between jurisdictions.

A more detailed summary of each chapter follows.

Chapter 1 introduces the concept of value, a fundamental metric of financial management. It covers key approaches to the measurement and understanding of value. The chapter further discusses financial modeling, which enables users to deal with multiple variables simultaneously and understand the impact of each variable on value.

Chapter 2 applies the concept of value to an examination of rules for decision-making on capital investments. Running a firm calls for decision-making on key investments, and this chapter describes the rules which guide the process from a financial perspective. It goes on to relate these rules to capability-building by firms.

Chapter 3 introduces the concept of asymmetric information in the financial markets. Dealing with uncertainty is an essential part of financial management, but equally important is an understanding of the asymmetries that prevail in the financial markets. These are themselves a source of uncertainty in the markets, and understanding their effect is key to sound financial management.

Chapter 4 covers decisions on capital structure. Given that firms fund their operations with capital provided by investors, a central concern is the combination of debt and equity that will form the capital structure. This chapter deals with the issues that arise from this choice. It also introduces the effect of the asymmetric information described in the previous chapter.

Chapter 5 deals with corporate mergers and acquisitions, including the divestitures which occur at the other end of an acquisition transaction. Mergers and acquisitions are executed based on corporate laws, and the chapter therefore discusses some legal aspects of transactions, including their structures and possible conflicts among parties.

Chapter 6 dedicates the whole chapter to the relationship between shareholders and stakeholders. Its importance is increasing ever, reflecting growing awareness toward a range of issues such as climate change and gender inequality. The chapter also relates to the next chapter dealing with various interests that are in conflict.

Finally, Chapter 7 discusses corporate governance. Corporate finance and corporate governance are flip sides of a coin in that managing capital provided by others creates a conflict by itself. Corporate governance is a system underlying firm activities, and the chapter discusses major issues in structuring it with an emphasis on comparative perspectives.

In totality, these chapters look at indispensable aspects of financial management as well as corporate governance of firms. We hope that readers will have better understandings of the structures and workings of firms and markets through them.

Chapter 1

Understanding Value

1. Overview

Value is the prime focus of a firm's financial management. As corporate value is usually measured in currency, value creation comprises a number of phenomena measured by their pecuniary value, such as profit-making, cash flow generation, and enhancement of stock market value. For a for-profit entity, value creation is a necessary condition for sustaining business. If such an entity fails to create value, it will need to shut down, because no one contributes financial or non-financial resources to a firm without expecting to be compensated for that contribution in a fair market. Even the mere prospect of future value enables a firm to fund its operations, invest the capital in assets, and hire people to realize its vision. Financial investors, such as shareholders and debtholders, are only able to profit from their investments if the firm succeeds in creating expected value. Therefore, sustainable value creation is the backbone of producers of goods and services. Created value enables firms and their investors to reinvest in further expansion or the creation of new businesses. Continuous value creation at the firm level leads to the growth of entire economies and financial markets, where firms and investors exchange and allocate resources for best use.

Even so, our society has a number of not-for-profit activities which do not aim to generate financial value. Such activities are typically financed by taxes and donations rather than corporate funding. But even when an activity is dedicated to a good cause, it will not be sustainable without good financial management and secure sources of incoming cash flow.

Non-governmental organizations, for instance, sometimes must downsize after failing to raise sufficient donations or control their cash outflow, and even the governments of some developing countries have been forced into default through poor financial management. Requirements for the financial viability of such entities do not differ from those for for-profit firms, which sustain themselves autonomously by financing investments and generating enough earnings for maintenance and growth. Financial management is thus an integral part of management for both for-profit and non-profit organizations.

In this book, "value" primarily means financial value. Focusing on financial value does not, of course, mean that it is the sole, gold standard. People do not invariably choose their careers according to relative potential income; they value other factors as well, such as their own professional aspirations, corporate culture, and work flexibility, some of which may well matter more than monetary considerations. In addition, there is a growing awareness that a corporation serves its set purpose, which is the raison d'etre of an enterprise.[1] From this perspective, managing and creating financial value are ways to serve the purpose of business rather than being its prime objective. We cover important trends in this area in Chapter 6.

To focus on financial value is to see the world through a monetary lens. Despite the diversifying notion of what value means, this lens gives us the advantage of understanding the world from a comprehensive and consistent perspective. This is because most of our activities involve the movement of cash: If we track the flow of money, we are most likely to comprehend what is really going on. Suppose we purchase a good from a firm. When we pay for it, cash goes out of our pocket into the firm, and the firm pays the costs necessary to produce the good, thus generating other streams of cash for employees, suppliers, and tax authorities. Similarly, if we decide to invest in a stock issued by a firm, cash again flows from us into the firm, which invests it to produce more goods, or to pay for its ongoing operations, prior to generating revenue. The firm may pay us dividends on our shares or buy them back in the future. All of these activities and transactions involve the flow of cash into and out of the firm.

---

[1]Mayer, C. (2018). *Prosperity: Better Business Makes the Greater Good.* Oxford, UK: Oxford University Press.

By viewing these activities through a monetary lens, we are given a coordinate axis by which to see and compare them and are better able to make informed and consistent decisions. The most important example of such consistency is seen in the market prices of goods and services, which are measured in financial value to convey their relative rarity in the marketplace. Given the function of market prices, entities such as firms, investors, managers, employees, suppliers, and governments commonly rely on this measure when making decisions bearing on the exchange of resources in a complex world. Stock price, for example, is a key piece of information on a firm. A stock price formed in the financial markets is a succinct reflection of the firm that issues it, enabling market participants to understand the firm and compare it with others with consistency. This is backed by the obvious fact that shares are tradable unless otherwise arranged by the firms involved. While firms can lock in capital contributed by shareholders and have discretion over its redistribution, shareholders are allowed to trade their holdings in the financial markets. This is a key feature of a corporation,[2] and it gives rise to the market prices of stocks in the financial markets.

2. Measuring Value

Let us take a closer look at financial value. Even for a single currency, value can be measured in various ways. It is necessary to make some distinctions even when dealing in one currency, as the value of a dollar, for example, will be different depending on the contexts and conditions that apply.

First, a dollar in the present is more valuable than a dollar in the future. This is because of the **time value of money**: A dollar in the present can add to value by earning interest between the two points of time, and so exceed the value of a dollar in the future. This can be made possible by investing the dollar in a government bond or an insured bank deposit that carries essentially no risk. A future dollar also carries **uncertainty**. While

---

[2]Armour, J., Hansmann, H., Kraakman, R., and Pargendler, M. (2017). What is corporate law? In R. Kraakman, J. Armour, P. Davies, L. Enriques, H. Hansmann, G. Hertig, H. Kanda, M. Pargendler, W. G. Ringe, and E. Rock (eds.), *The Anatomy of Corporate Law: A Comparative and Functional Approach*, 3rd ed. Oxford, UK: Oxford University Press, pp. 1–28.

a dollar in your hand is certain, you cannot know if you will have a future dollar until you actually have one in hand. This degree of uncertainty, or **risk**, causes a difference in value between the two. Since people usually dislike risk, they demand compensation for it in proportion to the degree of uncertainty. Such risk and compensation may be very small, as with the nominal interest rate given on safe bank deposits, or very large, as with the deep discounts demanded for stock in a near-bankrupt firm.

The need to compensate for the gap between present and future value, conditional upon uncertainty and the time value of money, creates the market price of capital. Price is a means used by the capital markets, or more broadly the financial markets, to inform people of the risk of their capital transactions. When people take on high risk, they get compensated with high return by paying a low price for their investment. The opposite is true when the risk taken on is low. Were this not the case, any investment offering high return relative to its risk would gather the attention of investors, and its price would be revised upward, thereby lowering the return, to reach an equilibrium in the financial markets. Similarly, any investment offering low return relative to risk would be sold, and its price revised downward, thereby increasing the return and reaching an equilibrium.

Under equilibrium, investors know the level of financial return they can expect when they invest their capital. This creates an **opportunity cost of capital**, which is the financial return that investors obtain, or at least know that they can obtain. When people invest in a specific firm or project, they form expectations by referring to information on the prices and returns of similar firms or projects in the financial markets, which they will have to give up when they choose one over another. Similarly, a firm that deploys capital is expected to generate a return equivalent to one that would be offered by other firms with equivalent risks. The required rate of return, or cost of capital, reflects a well-functioning market that informs investors and firms of the price of risk in the trade of capital.

3. The Capital Asset Pricing Model

A standard measure for setting a required return is the **capital asset pricing model (CAPM)**. Devised in the 1960s,[3] it provides a way to derive a

---

[3] Sharpe, W. F. (1964). Capital asset prices: A theory of market equilibrium under conditions of risk. *Journal of Finance*, 19(3), 425–442; Lintner, J. (1965). The valuation of risk

required rate of return by assessing the risk of an individual stock, measured as **beta**, relative to the overall market. A beta is calculated by dividing the covariance between the returns of a stock and the overall market by the variance of returns in the overall market, both of which are obtained from historical data. The overall market, or the *market*, typically refers to widely available, liquid stock indices, such as the S&P 500 in the U.S., although conceptually it should be the entire market available in all countries.

3.1. Beta

A beta indicates the sensitivity of an asset, such as stock, to the overall market. A beta of one means that the risk is equivalent to that of the overall market, whereas a beta which is larger (smaller) than one means that the stock moves more (less) than the overall market, indicating a higher (lower) risk. The idea of the CAPM is that the risk of a stock, or more generally all investable assets, is in proportion to its beta. It also assumes that risk and return are linearly correlated and that the expected return of a stock is unambiguously determined by its beta when the expected return of the overall market is given. Since the CAPM uses only one variable, the beta, to calculate required rate of return, it is also called the single-factor model.

Let us calculate a beta in practice. Table 1.1 shows annual stock returns of the S&P 500 (x_i) and JPMorgan Chase (y_i). The average return of the S&P 500 (μ_x) is 12.2 percent, and that of JPMorgan (μ_y) is 12.5 percent. The table shows the difference between the returns for each year and their average, which are ($x_i - \mu_x$) for the S&P 500, and ($y_i - \mu_y$) for JPMorgan. The covariance between the S&P 500 and JPMorgan is obtained by dividing the sum of the products of the differences, expressed as ($x_i - \mu_x$)($y_i - \mu_y$), by the number of data points minus one, which is 10 in this case. The subtraction of one is to reflect the statistical property that the data are a sample from a limited period of time; otherwise we need only to divide the sum by the total number of data points, 11 in this case.

assets and the selection of risky investments in stock portfolios and capital budgets. *Review of Economics and Statistics*, 47(1), 13–37; Mossin, J. (1966). Equilibrium in a capital asset market. *Econometrica*, 34(4), 768–783.

Table 1.1   Calculating beta.

	x_i	μ_x	$x_i - \mu_x$	y_i	μ_y	$y_i - \mu_y$	$(x_i - \mu_x)$ $(y_i - \mu_y)$
2010	12.8%	12.2%	0.6%	1.8%	12.5%	−10.7%	−0.1%
2011	0.0%	12.2%	−12.2%	−21.6%	12.5%	−34.1%	4.2%
2012	13.4%	12.2%	1.2%	32.2%	12.5%	19.7%	0.2%
2013	29.6%	12.2%	17.4%	33.0%	12.5%	20.5%	3.6%
2014	11.4%	12.2%	−0.8%	7.0%	12.5%	−5.5%	0.0%
2015	−0.7%	12.2%	−12.9%	5.5%	12.5%	−7.0%	0.9%
2016	9.5%	12.2%	−2.7%	30.7%	12.5%	18.2%	−0.5%
2017	19.4%	12.2%	7.2%	23.9%	12.5%	11.4%	0.8%
2018	−6.2%	12.2%	−18.5%	−8.7%	12.5%	−21.2%	3.9%
2019	28.9%	12.2%	16.7%	42.8%	12.5%	30.3%	5.0%
2020	16.3%	12.2%	4.1%	−8.9%	12.5%	−21.4%	−0.9%
Sum							17.3%
COVARIANCE.S		1.7%		VAR.S for x_i		1.3%	
CORREL		0.71		VAR.S for y_i		4.5%	
β		1.32					

Since the sum of the products is 17.3 percent, the covariance is 17.3/10 = 1.7 percent.

The same result is obtained by using spreadsheet software. Excel® calculates the same value with the COVARIANCE.S function, by which inputs of the two sets of time-series data, x_i and y_i in this case, return the value of covariance as an output. The "S" in the function indicates that the data are a sample.

To obtain a beta, we then calculate the variance of the S&P 500. Since the variance is a special case of covariance in which x_i equals y_i, we need only to divide the sum of the products $(x_i - \mu_x)(x_i - \mu_x)$, or a square of $(x_i - \mu_x)$, by 10, which is again the number of samples minus one. The result is 1.3 percent, which is also obtained by applying the VAR.S function of Excel to the data set of x_i.

Now that we have both the covariance between the S&P 500 and JPMorgan and the variance of the S&P 500, we finally obtain the beta of JPMorgan by dividing the former with the latter, resulting in

1.7/1.3 = 1.32. The result indicates that the stock of JPMorgan is more volatile than the overall market; when the market moves by 1 percent point in either direction, it moves by 1.32 percent in the same direction.

The idea of relative sensitivity makes correlation a key metric. Indicating how closely one stock moves in relation to another, it normalizes covariance between a stock and the overall market. It is obtained by dividing the covariance by each of the standard deviations of the stock and the overall market. By virtue of normalization, correlation ranges from minus one to plus one. Even if a stock's relative volatility is high, a low correlation offsets the risk, resulting in a relatively low beta. A beta of one (zero) corresponds to a correlation of one (zero). In the above example, the standard deviation of x_i is obtained by taking a root of the variance, which is $1.3\%^{1/2} = 11.5$ percent; by the same calculation, that of y_i is obtained as $4.5\%^{1/2} = 21.1$ percent. The same results for standard deviations are obtained by applying the STDEV.S function of Excel to each set of data points. The correlation between the S&P 500 and JPMorgan is thus 0.017/0.115/0.211 = 0.72. The same result is obtained by applying the CORREL function of Excel to the two sets of data points. This indicates that, while the relative volatility of JPMorgan is high at 21.1 percent versus 11.5 percent for the overall market, the correlation of less than one at 0.72 moderates the riskiness, resulting in a beta of 1.32, or $0.211/0.115 \times 0.72$.

3.2. The model

Now that we have a beta, we proceed to obtain the required rate of return. The idea of the CAPM is that the required rate of return of a stock (or more generally, an asset) is proportional to its beta as follows:

$$r_i \cong \beta(r_m \quad r_f) \quad r_f$$

where r_i is the required rate of return of a stock i, β is its beta, r_m is the overall market return, and r_f is the risk-free rate. When the market return, which is the return of the S&P 500, and the risk-free rate, which is the return on a government bond, are given, only a beta determines the required rate of return of a stock.

The formula is graphically expressed in Figure 1.1. This is called the **security market line (SML)**, and shows that the relationship is linear.

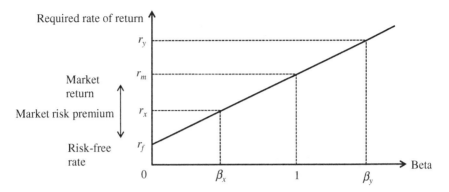

Figure 1.1   Security market line.

When a beta is equal to one, the required return is the same as the market return (r_m). A smaller beta (β_x) results in a lower return (r_x) than the market return, and a larger beta (β_y) results in a higher return (r_y), as is the case with the JPMorgan stock. A beta of zero means that the asset is risk-free, and the required rate is the same as the risk-free rate (r_f). The difference between the market return and the risk-free rate ($r_m - r_f$) is called the **market risk premium**, which is the compensation required for taking on the risk of the overall market expressed as the rate of return. Investors add this premium to the risk-free rate when taking on the risk of the overall market.

For example, let us say that the market risk premium ($r_m - r_f$) is 5 percent and the risk-free rate (r_f) is 2 percent. The required market return is (5% + 2%) = 7%. By applying the beta of 1.32 to the CAPM formula, we obtain a required rate of return of 1.32 × (7% − 2%) + 2% = 8.6 percent. Alternatively, if we multiply the market risk premium by the beta to obtain the premium over the risk-free rate required for the JPMorgan stock, the required rate of return is (1.32 × 5% + 2%) = 8.6 percent.

While the CAPM is clear in its definition of the beta and the formula that incorporates it, it leaves much to market practice when it comes to the choice of market return and risk-free rate. Market return is often estimated by taking an arithmetic average of historical market returns. Similarly, market risk premium is estimated based on an average of the differences between the market return and the risk-free rate. Research estimates that the premium over short-term bills is between 4 and 6 percent, and that over long-term bonds is between 3 and 5 percent.[4] The required premium is also estimated by periodically conducting a survey of real-world managers who actually make investment and financing decisions.[5] The risk-free rate is obtained from the latest bond market data at the time a required rate of return is calculated. While it is consistent to match the term of a bond with the investment horizon of a stock, yields on 10-year or 30-year government bonds are often adopted in practice because they have a liquid market and their prices reflect more information than those in a less liquid market.

While the CAPM assumes that a beta is stable as long as a firm's risk is unchanged relative to the overall market, in reality it is not. This indicates that the variability of stock performance is greater than that of a firm's intrinsic business over time, reflecting changing market sentiments toward the risks and prospects of individual firms. To complement the inevitable variability, investors often refer to an industry average of competing firms, which is more stable in that the fluctuations of individual stocks are offset against one another.

3.3. Alternative models

While the CAPM has been the standard model used in estimating a required cost of capital, its validity has been the subject of debate. The actual returns of low-beta firms tend to be higher than the model predicts, while the opposite holds true for high-beta firms.[6] It is also found that some **multi-factor models** have more predicative power than the CAPM, although it remains theoretically unclear why that is the case, and this relationship may fade as these models are adopted by market participants. The contribution of the CAPM lies in its establishing a risk–return relationship by introducing a single risk factor with a theoretical clarity that competing models fail to match. Nevertheless, since alternative multi-factor models more closely accord with actual returns, they coexist with the CAPM in practice even if not overriding it.

---

[4] Welch, I. (2000). Views of financial economists on the equity premium and on professional controversies. *Journal of Business*, 73(4), 501–537.

[5] Graham, J. R. and Harvey, C. R. (2005). The long-run equity risk premium. *Finance Research Letters*, 2(4), 185–194.

[6] Black, F. (1993). Beta and return. *Journal of Portfolio Management*, 20(4), 8–18.

The most important multi-factor model adopts three factors: market risk premium; return on small-firm stocks less return on large-firm stocks; and return on high book-to-market stocks less return on low book-to-market stocks.[7] A four-factor model, which further adds a momentum factor obtained using the return from investing in top-ranked firms in a prior year while short-selling bottom-ranked ones, is widely used in assessing the performance of portfolio investments.[8] However, the use of these alternative models is limited to the field of investment management, and it is fair to say that the CAPM is still the dominant model for estimating required rate of return in corporate settings.

There is another function where the CAPM performs less than optimally, and this is in the valuation of startups. Given the high level of uncertainty faced by startups and their investors, a future cash flow or operating metric is often discounted with a very high rate of return. It is not unusual, for instance, to apply a required rate of return of 40–50 percent, which is inconsistent with the idea of the CAPM. This indicates that the model fits well with firms that have a relatively stable cash flow, but less well with those featuring high uncertainty, such as fledgling startups aiming for a public listing. For the latter, a relative valuation using multiples of sales or other drivers is adopted instead, as we shall see in the next chapter.

3.4. Weighted Average Cost of Capital

The CAPM and the other models are primarily applied in estimating required rate of return on equity. However, if a firm chooses to finance its operations with a combination of debt and equity, the firm-level rate of return, or cost of capital, consists of a mix of the two. In this case, it is necessary to estimate a firm-wide cost of capital by averaging the costs of debt and equity capital.

Figure 1.2 explains the idea of averaging using a firm's market-value balance sheet. Unlike a standard balance sheet, which is book-value based, the market-value balance sheet expresses the current value of the

---

[7]Fama, E. F. and French, K. R. (1995). Size and book-to-market factors in earnings and returns. *Journal of Finance*, 50(1), 131–155.

[8]Carhart, M. M. (1997). On persistence in mutual fund performance. *Journal of Finance*, 52(1), 57–82.

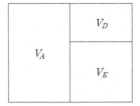

Figure 1.2 Market-value balance sheet of a firm.

firm's assets, debt, and equity. Typically, short-term debt is offset against short-term assets in order to focus on the long-term capital deployed by the firm. As is the case with a book-value based balance sheet, the market-value based sheet balances so that the market value of the firm's assets, or firm value, equals the sum of the market value of its debt and equity. That is:

$$\ddot{u}_{\ddot{u}} = \quad +$$

where V_A is firm value, V_D is debt value, and V_E is equity value.

Debt and equity require different costs of capital reflecting their difference in risk. When a firm uses both sources, the average cost that it faces vis-à-vis investors is the weighted average of those costs. This is called the **weighted average cost of capital (WACC)**:

$$r_{WACC} = r_D \left(1 - t\right)\frac{V_D}{V_A} + r_E \frac{V_E}{V_A}$$

where r_{WACC} is the after-tax weighted average cost of capital, t is corporate tax rate, r_D is the debt cost of capital, and r_E is the equity cost of capital. Suppose that a firm's equity has the same level of risk as JPMorgan, which has an equity cost of capital of 8.6 percent, and that the firm finances a quarter of its operations through debt and the remaining three quarters through equity. If the debt cost of capital is 3 percent, which is the rate of return at which a firm is currently able to issue a bond, and the corporate tax rate is 30 percent, the firm's after-tax debt cost is 3 × (1 − 30%) = 2.1 percent, reflecting the tax deductibility of interest expenses. In this case, the firm's WACC is (8.6% × 3/4 + 2.1% × 1/4) = 7.0 percent. This is a firm-wide cost of capital that reflects its mix of different sources of capital and the overall risk of its assets. We shall see more about the WACC in Chapter 4 in relation to capital structure.

These models and formulae for estimating the required rate of return for investment and financing derive from the need to obtain a value that accurately reflects differences in the risk and timing of cash flow. In other words, the rate of return connects a present dollar and a future dollar. Now that we have an appropriate measure of the required rate of return, we proceed to estimate the cash flow to which the rate is applied.

4. Cash Flow

With the required rate of return, the straightforward procedure is to obtain the **present value** of cash flow based on an estimate of future cash flow.[9] Since future cash flow is uncertain and carries risk, the **discount rate** reflects this and is set higher than the risk-free rate.

The value of a firm is seen as the present value of the **free cash flow** it is expected to generate in the future. Free cash flow is the amount of cash that a firm has at hand after collecting revenues from selling its goods and services, paying for necessary expenses such as ingredients, labor, and advertising, and investing in new facilities and equipment and otherwise maintaining and expanding its operations. While it would be most precise to predict, item by item, the exact amount of cash a firm collects and pays in the course of its business, future free cash flow is typically estimated as a pro forma derived from projected financial statements. It is defined as follows:

$$FCF = EBIT(1 - t) + Depreciation - Capex - \Delta NWC$$

where FCF is free cash flow, EBIT is **earnings before interest and taxes (EBIT)**, t is corporate tax rate, *Depreciation* is depreciation and amortization, *Capex* is capital expenditure, and ΔNWC is a year-on-year increase in net working capital. EBIT $(1 - t)$ is also called **net operating profit after taxes (NOPAT)**.

Notice that EBIT $(1 - t)$, or NOPAT, is independent of a firm's interest expenses. This means that free cash flow is independent of a firm's degree

---

[9]Williams, J. B. (1938). *The Theory of Investment Value*. Cambridge, MA: Harvard University Press.

of leverage. Corporate tax is therefore a constructive amount that can actually be lowered through a tax deduction if the firm has paid interest. We make this construction in order to assess the level of cash flow unaffected by the choice of leverage. This is helpful in estimating intrinsic business value regardless of financial decisions on leverage.

Depreciation and amortization are non-cash expenses linked to capital expenditure. Accounting principles allow firms to allocate capital expenditures such as facilities and equipment over the years that they are in use, and thereby level the costs of large onetime expenditures. However, since we are interested in real cash flow without this leveling effect, we add back depreciation and amortization to derive free cash flow. We choose instead to deduct the amount of capital expenditure, since cash payments are made at the time of investment even if not immediately expensed on the book.

Increases in net working capital are also regarded as real cash outflow even if not expensed on the book. Net working capital is typically defined as the sum of the amounts of accounts receivable and inventory less the amount of accounts payable. An increase in NWC occurs when a firm (i) increases the amount of accounts receivable, indicating an increase in sales with cash payment still pending and resulting in a decrease in cash relative to booked sales; (ii) increases the amount of inventory, indicating pre-sales investment in inventory and resulting in a decrease in cash; or (iii) decreases the amount of accounts payable, indicating settlement of a deferred payment and resulting in a decrease in cash. In contrast, a decrease in net working capital occurs when a firm collects its receivables early, reduces its inventory, or defers its payment, all of which increases its cash and thus its free cash flow.

Let us see how this works in practice. Table 1.2 shows the financial projections of a firm that manufactures widgets. In Year 3, for instance, its free cash flow is calculated as $(136 + 154 - 169 - 10) = 111$, in million dollars, given its projected EBIT, depreciation and amortization, capital expenditure, and net working capital. We assume that the firm's **operating margin**, which is operating earnings divided by sales, is 15 percent and that the corporate tax rate is 30 percent. Depreciation and amortization tend to increase because the firm is increasing its capital expenditure in line with the growth of its sales. Despite the increase in the firm's investments, its free cash flow is increasing as well, as the growth of its earnings and the addback of depreciation and amortization surpass the increase in investments.

Table 1.2　Free cash flow.

Year	1	2	3	4	5
1 Sales	1,200	1,248	1,298	1,350	1,404
2 (Operating expenses)	−1,020	−1,061	−1,103	−1,147	−1,193
3 EBIT (1 − 2)	180	187	195	202	211
4 (Taxes)	−54	−56	−58	−61	−63
5 EBIT (1 − t) (3 − 4)	126	131	136	142	147
6 Depreciation/Amortization	142	148	154	160	166
7 Capital expenditure	156	162	169	175	182
8 Net working capital	210	219	229	237	247
9 ΔNWC	10	9	10	8	10
10 FCF (5 + 6 − 7 − 9)	102	108	111	119	122
Discount factor	0.93	0.87	0.82	0.76	0.71
Present value	95	94	91	91	87

Since free cash flow is the amount of cash available after a firm invests in maintenance and expansion, it is available either for retention within the firm or for distribution to its investors. For distribution, it can be used to repay debt, pay dividends, or repurchase shares. It is "free" in the sense that it is freely available to the investors that contribute capital to the firm for its business operations.

In this respect, it is sometimes argued in policy discussions that firms should be restricted from paying dividends and repurchasing shares, as they could use these funds to spend more on people, research and development, and capital investments for the future rather than on short-term benefits for investors.[10] When managers are assessed based on short-term performance, they may be inclined to reduce investments and expenditures in order to meet an earnings target, even if this may harm the firm's profitability in the long run. Indeed, there is evidence that managers will actually cut investments to meet annual earnings targets.[11] Since an increase in costs will make their firm appear to be underperforming

---

[10]Lazonick, W. (2014). Profit without prosperity. *Harvard Business Review*, September 1, 2014.

[11]Graham, J. R., Harvey, C. R., and Rajgopal, S. (2005). The economic implications of corporate financial reporting. *Journal of Accounting and Economics*, 40(1–3), 3–73.

vis-à-vis its peers, managers may not maintain a long-term perspective if they are constantly assessed on the basis of single-year performance, especially in a competitive context.

However, restricting payouts will not cure such short-termism, if such a cure even exists. Such arguments often overlook the fact that when seen as a whole in the financial markets, firms procure capital on the one hand while paying it out on the other, resulting in only moderate net payouts. Evidence also shows that in aggregate, firms' capital expenditure and research and development expenses exceed net payouts to shareholders.[12] Excess cash distributed by firms to their investors goes on to be reinvested in other firms that need cash for their own operation and growth. This means that capital otherwise held by a firm flows to others, possibly for more productive uses, and there is no point that a firm holds, or dares to make unproductive use of, redundant capital left after funding its operations and making necessary investments for growth. While the calculation of free cash flow appears mechanical, it reflects firms' investment and payout policies and even becomes a subject for policy discussion.

Calculating the free cash flow of the firm for each year, it is now possible to obtain the present value of future cash flow. Suppose that the required rate of return, or discount rate, for the future cash flow of the firm is 7 percent, which is equal to the WACC derived in the previous section. The free cash flow in, say, Year 3 is 111, and its present value is calculated by discounting it at 7 percent, compounded, or $111/1.07^3 = 91$. It is often useful to apply a discount factor, which is a coefficient for converting a future value to a present value. For Year 3, it is $1/1.07^3$, or 0.82. Similarly, the present values of free cash flow for Years 1, 2, 4, and 5 are calculated as 95, 94, 91, and 87, respectively, by applying the discount factors of 0.93, 0.87, 0.76, and 0.71.

Here, the present value of 91 is equivalent to the future value of 111 in Year 3, so a promise to receive free cash flow of 111 in Year 3 is traded at 91 at present. At a level of expectation, an investment in the promise to receive 111 in Year 3 for 91 would earn a return of 7 percent, compounded. This is a fair deal because the rate reflects a market where investors could earn 7 percent by investing in other firms with similar risks. Since it carries uncertainty, it might be the case that the firm actually generates more or less than 111, resulting in a rate of return for investors

---

[12]Fried, J. M. and Wang, C. C. Y. (2021). Short-termism, shareholder payouts, and investment in the EU. *European Financial Management*, 27(3), 389–413.

which is different from the expected rate. These *ex post* results lead investors to update their assessment of the firm in either direction. It also affects the opportunity cost of capital in the whole financial market by updating information held by market participants.

Repeating the same exercise, a promise to receive the firm's free cash flow throughout the next five years is valued at 458, which is the sum of the present value of the five streams of free cash flow, each discounted at 7 percent, compounded.

5. Valuing a Firm

Let us proceed to obtain the value of a whole firm by applying the same method of discounting future cash flow. A firm is usually operated on the assumption of its being a **going concern**, meaning that it will continue to operate in perpetuity. In reality, however, corporations vanish by being sold, merged, or dissolved, while new ones come into life with new people, ideas, and technologies. The oldest known firm in the world is Kongo-Gumi, a Japanese builder of wooden temples and shrines that was founded in the 6th century.[13] Despite the low probability of survival over centuries, the assumption of **perpetuity** accords with valuation practice because, through the effect of compounded discounting, the further a future cash flow is from the present, the less relevant it is to the present value. In contrast, if plans call for a project or firm to be operated for a specific period and then liquidated, there is no problem in limiting its free cash flow projection to that period and discounting it accordingly.

Under the assumption of perpetuity, firm value is calculated as the value of free cash flow with a constant **growth rate**. The present value of such a growing perpetuity is expressed as follows:

$$V = \frac{\text{FCF}}{r - g}$$

where FCF is the free cash flow of a firm one year from the time of valuation, r is the required rate of return, or the discount rate, that reflects the risk of the free cash flow, and g is the growth rate of the free cash flow.

---

[13] Pilling, D. (2007). Kongo Gumi: Building a future on the past. *Financial Times*, October 19, 2007.

When the free cash flow is constant, g is equal to zero. The setting of one year from the time of valuation is mostly for expediency as it fits into a formula for the sum of a geometric progression.[14]

Using the example in Table 1.2, let us calculate the value of free cash flow in Year 6 and thereafter (terminal value) by assuming that free cash flow is expected to grow at a rate of 3 percent annually. In that case, the value of free cash flow in Year 6 and thereafter (terminal value), calculated at the time of Year 5, is $122(1.03)/(7\% - 3\%) = 3,136$. The numerator, the free cash flow in Year 6, is 122 times 1.03, reflecting the growth by 3 percent from the cash flow in Year 5. The denominator is the difference between the required cost of capital and the growth rate. The present value, or the value in Year 0, is $3,136/1.07^5 = 2,236$, obtained by discounting the value at the time of Year 5 by five years. If it is reasonable to assume that growth rates vary, as seen in the trajectory of a growth firm with a period of high growth followed by one of low growth, we split the periods accordingly and calculate the value of free cash flow during each period.

To complete the valuation in Table 1.2, we add the value of the growing perpetuity, 2,236, to the present value of free cash flow from Years 1 through 5, 458, making 2,694, which is the value of the whole firm, or firm value. This method of obtaining value by discounting a firm's future free cash flow is called the **discounted cash flow (DCF)** method. The DCF method consists of projections of free cash flow and estimates of required rate of return and growth rate, and is the standard method used to value firms.

The method essentially capitalizes *flow* to obtain the value of *stock*. In simple form, the value of stock, V, is the value of flow, C, divided by a required rate, r, or $V = C/r$. The stock generates an annual return of V times r, or C, which is the value of flow. Since the rate to capitalize flow is implied in the price of stock, price information in the financial markets is indispensable in valuing firms. As the stock price continues to change through trades in the markets reflecting demand and supply, so does the implied rate of return. This means that the value of a firm continues to change as well, reflecting the state of the markets that value it, even if its own cash flow projection is constant.

---

[14]Multiplying by $\frac{1+g}{1+r}$ the both sides of an equation $V = \frac{FCF}{(1+r)} + \frac{FCF(1+g)}{(1+r)^2} + \frac{FCF(1+g)^2}{(1+r)^3} + \dots$, we obtain $\frac{V(1+g)}{(1+r)} = \frac{FCF(1+g)}{(1+r)^2} + \frac{FCF(1+g)^2}{(1+r)^3} + \frac{FCF(1+g)^3}{(1+r)^4} + \dots$. From the two equations, $V - \frac{V(1+g)}{(1+r)} = \frac{FCF}{(1+r)}$. Hence, $\frac{(1+r)V - V(1+g)}{(1+r)} = \frac{FCF}{(1+r)}$, or, $V = \frac{FCF}{r-g}$.

5.1. Equity value

Since firm value is ultimately distributed to debt or equity holders, we obtain the equity value of a firm by subtracting debt value from firm value. This is clear from the market-value balance sheet already shown in Figure 1.2. Since it is its total assets that generate a firm's free cash flow, the present value of free cash flow is equal to the market value of the total assets. Although free cash flow is available for distribution to debt and equity investors, debtholders have priority over shareholders regarding the distribution of value. Reflecting this priority, equity value is the residual value after subtracting debt value, or $V_E = V_A - V_D$.

Let us see an example by continuing the valuation of the firm in Table 1.2, whose result is shown in Table 1.3. If the firm finances a quarter of its capital through debt, as assumed in deriving the WACC, the value of the debt is 2,694/4, or 674. The equity value is then (2,694 − 674) = 2,020. If we additionally assume that the number of shares outstanding is 100, in millions, we ultimately obtain a per-share value of 2,020/100, or $20.2.

Note that debt value is the value of *net* debt. This is the amount of debt left after subtracting the amount of cash and equivalent liquidity, as a firm is able to redeem its debt with such liquidity whenever it wants. When a firm still carries excess liquidity even after subtracting all its debt, the value of equity is the sum of the value of operating assets and that of excess liquidity, as shareholders are entitled to a stake in not only the firm's operating assets but also its excess liquidity. However, the amount

Table 1.3 Valuation summary.

Discount rate	7%		6%	7%	8%
Growth rate	3%	2%	2,791	2,229	1,853
Terminal value in Year 5	3,136	3%	3,594	2,694	2,152
PV of 5-year FCF	458	4%	5,202	3,468	2,599
PV of terminal value	2,236				
Firm value	2,694				
Debt value	674				
Equity value	2,020				
# of shares outstanding	100				
Value per share	20.2				

of cash essential for a firm's operation, such as cash stored in cash registers by retail outlets, should not be offset against debt but be counted as a part of operating assets.

To summarize these exercises, we now see that the value of equity is the present value of a firm's future free cash flow less the value of net debt, and that a share price is a slice of the equity value divided by the number of shares outstanding. The rate of return required to discount the future value into the present one is the opportunity cost of capital determined in the financial markets. It reflects the risk of a firm's equity relative to the overall market. The WACC is appropriate as a discount rate for a firm's free cash flow because it applies to cash flowing from the whole of the firm's activities and reflects its overall risk.

5.2. Sensitivity analysis

As we have seen, the valuation process requires a number of assumptions. It is helpful, therefore, to comprehend the sensitivity of firm value to those inputs. A **sensitivity analysis** serves this purpose, appearing in Table 1.3 as a matrix of key assumptions and the values that correspond to them. The table gives an example of the sensitivity of firm value to assumptions of discount rate (horizontal axis) and growth rate (vertical axis).

Because it offers a range of outputs under possible inputs, a sensitivity analysis is helpful in discerning possible value from impossible value. Understanding reasonable range is important given that firm value can be elusive, as it depends on the perception of participants in the financial markets who value firms based on their own positions and assumptions. While the table shows a standard choice of two variables, there could be others, such as a firm's profit margin, the timing of free cash flow linked to a planned product launch, or capital expenditure and net working capital requirements, each of which is affected by a firm's operating environment and position. These variables are called **value drivers** in the sense that they are key inputs driving firm value. It is a manager's responsibility to identify, track, and improve these drivers for the successful growth of firm value.

6. Financial Modeling

A firm's free cash flow is derived from its future projections. As we saw in the previous section, such projections are usually expressed in the language of accounting. It is useful, therefore, to understand the basic workings of financial statements and their relation to free cash flow through financial modeling. A financial model also provides a consistency check for projections, making sure that there is no discrepancy among variables.

The three major financial statements used in a financial model are the balance sheet, the income statement, and the cash flow statement. These are shown in Tables 1.4 through 1.6, which are based on the example of the previous section. In principle, a firm's activities are reflected in the income statement and the cash flow statement as *flow*, and in the balance sheet as *stock*. These are linked to each other and require consistency under shared assumptions. For the purpose of valuation, it is helpful to view these statements from two perspectives: investment and financing.

6.1. Investment

Let us start with investment. A firm makes a number of capital investments for its business, such as building factories, retail stores and

Table 1.4 Balance sheet.

Year	1	2	3	4	5
Cash/Securities	163	159	157	163	172
Accounts receivable	180	187	195	202	211
Inventory	163	170	177	184	191
Fixed assets	1,614	1,628	1,643	1,658	1,674
Total assets	2,120	2,144	2,173	2,208	2,248
Accounts payable	133	138	143	149	155
Long-term debt	674	674	674	674	674
Net assets	1,313	1,332	1,356	1,385	1,419
Debt and net assets	2,120	2,144	2,173	2,208	2,248
Accounts receivable/Sales	15%	15%	15%	15%	15%
Inventory/Op. expenses	16%	16%	16%	16%	16%
Accounts payable/Op. expenses	13%	13%	13%	13%	13%

Table 1.5   Income statement.

Year	1	2	3	4	5
Sales	1,200	1,248	1,298	1,350	1,404
Operating expenses:					
Depreciation/amortization	−142	−148	−154	−160	−166
Other expenses	−878	−913	−949	−987	−1,027
Operating profits	180	187	195	202	211
Earnings on securities	2	2	2	2	2
Interest expenses	−20	−20	−20	−20	−20
Pretax earnings	162	169	177	184	193
Taxes	−49	−51	−53	−55	−58
Net income	113	118	124	129	135

Table 1.6   Cash flow statement.

Year	1	2	3	4	5
CF from operating activities:					
Pretax earnings	162	169	177	184	193
(+) Depreciation/amortization	142	148	154	160	166
(−) Increase in NWC	−10	−9	−10	−8	−10
(−) Taxes	−49	−51	−53	−55	−58
Total	245	257	267	281	291
CF from investing activities:					
(−) Capital expenditure	−156	−162	−169	−175	−182
Total	−156	−162	−169	−175	−182
CF from financing activities:					
(+) Borrowing/repayment	0	0	0	0	0
(+) Share issuance/repurchase	−100	−100	−100	−100	−100
Total	−100	−100	−100	−100	−100
(+) Change in cash	−11	−5	−2	6	9
NOPAT	126	131	136	142	147
FCF	102	108	111	119	122
(Reconciliation)	102	108	111	119	122

warehouses and purchasing computers, software and patents. These are long-term investments that build a basis for operations. The capital investments made by a firm increase the fixed assets on its balance sheet, which decrease, except for land, through depreciation and amortization.

Table 1.4 shows that fixed assets at the end of Year 3 are 1,643. This is the result of capital expenditure of 169 and depreciation and amortization of 154 in the same year, producing a net increase of 15 over the previous year's balance, which is recorded as 1,628. The same amount of depreciation and amortization appears on the income statement in Table 1.5 as part of operating expenses. Any capital investments lead to an increase in depreciation and amortization during the period over which the investments are depreciated and amortized. The period allowed for depreciation and amortization does not necessarily match the actual period in which an asset is in use because the former is defined by accounting standards and tax codes.

Depreciation and amortization have the effect of reducing taxable income and thus taxes. For instance, when the firm in the example depreciates and amortizes its assets by 154, it reduces taxable income by the same amount, and thus taxes by $154 \times 30\%$, assuming a corporate tax rate of 30 percent, even if the depreciation and amortization are a non-cash expense. This means that the net cost of an investment is less than its face value according to the tax rate by virtue of tax savings received afterward. To enjoy the time value of such tax savings, a firm will generally depreciate and amortize an asset as early as possible within the limit of applicable tax codes.

The cash flow statement in Table 1.6 adds back depreciation and amortization in order to reverse the decrease in earnings to calculate the cash flow (CF) from operating activities on the cash flow statement. It also reflects the capital expenditure of 169 as part of the cash flow (CF) from investment activities, which the income statement does not reflect except for the amount of its depreciation and amortization during the same year. When a firm grows, capital expenditure tends to be larger than depreciation and amortization, indicating that the firm is expanding its asset base to support its growth.

Firms also invest in net working capital, which is calculated as the sum of the amounts of accounts receivable and inventory less that of accounts payable. These are short-term investments that support a firm's day-to-day operations. In the financial model, the requirement for net working capital is linked to the firm's sales and operating expenses.

Table 1.4 makes the assumptions that accounts receivable are 15 percent of sales, and inventory and accounts payable are respectively 16 percent and 13 percent of operating expenses. These ratios reflect the firm's trading circumstances. For example, the input of 15 percent of sales means that the firm actually collects cash on an average of 365 days $\times$ 15% = 55 days after booking a sale. Similarly, the inputs on inventory and accounts receivable mean that the firm pays its expenses on an average of 365 days $\times$ 13% = 47 days after it makes purchases, and puts its goods on the shelf for an average period of 365 days $\times$ 16% = 58 days.

The difference among these variables creates gaps between cash outflows and inflows, requiring the firm to continually invest cash in order to fill them in. For instance, the net working capital in Year 3 is (195 + 177 − 143) = 229. Reflecting the firm's growth in both sales and purchasing, the amount increases over the previous year by 10, from 219 to 229. To support the growth, the firm needs to make additional investment of 10, which decreases its free cash flow for the year. While the income statement does not reflect this investment, the cash flow statement does, by decreasing the cash flow from operating activities by the same amount, as shown in Table 1.6.

These gaps also indicate the relative bargaining power of the firms involved. A firm may be able to improve its cash flow by negotiating better terms with its customers and suppliers and by making inventory management more efficient by coordinating the timing of deliveries with its suppliers. Better terms for one party often imply a burden for the counterparty, such as carrying inventory on its own shelves in place of its customer's. A dominant retailer often has a negative net working capital requirement, meaning that it collects cash from its customers even before it pays its suppliers for the sold goods. Because the required investment in its net working capital declines, the retailer can increase its free cash flow even as it expands its operations.

To summarize, a firm's capital investments appear as fixed assets on the balance sheet and as cash outflow on the cash flow statement. They increase the depreciation and amortization that appear as expenses on the income statement and reduce the amount of fixed assets on the balance sheet, while in the cash flow statement their expensing is reversed as a non-cash item. Net working capital investment appears on the balance sheet as accounts receivable, inventory, and accounts payable, driven by operating activities that appear on the income statement as sales and operating expenses. An increase in net working capital is reflected in the cash flow statement as an adjustment to the earnings in the income statement, which does not reflect the investment in net working capital. These entries and adjustments are mutually consistent, and express the state of the firm's business.

6.2. Financing

Let us proceed to the financing which supports a firm's investments. Financing consists mainly of debt and equity. Continuing the same example, suppose that the firm has long-term debt of 674, which is equivalent to a quarter of its firm value of 2,696. We assume in the model that the debt has a maturity of more than five years, meaning that its balance is constant over the projected period. The interest rate on the debt is 3 percent, and the interest expenses of $674 \times 3\%$, or 20, appear on the income statement in Table 1.5. After-tax interest expenses are lower at $20 \times (1 - 30\%) = 14$, reflecting the tax deductibility of interest expenses.

As another means of financing, the firm can issue shares. It can also finance its investments internally by retaining part of its earnings. For instance, the cash flow from operating activities in Year 3, which appears on the cash flow statement in Table 1.6, indicates that the firm generates cash flow of 267 while its investment needs, which are shown in the cash flow from investing activities, are less than that at 169. Unless the firm has a need to accumulate its cash holdings, this will give rise to a redundancy of cash. Absent such a need, the firm distributes the cash by either paying dividends or repurchasing shares. We assume here that the firm repurchases shares in the amount of 100.

By distributing the redundant cash to investors, the firm keeps its cash balance roughly constant, which is reflected in the relatively small change in the cash balance shown at the bottom of the cash flow statement. This change is equal to that on the balance sheet. In Year 3, for instance, the amount of cash and securities on the balance sheet in Table 1.4 decreases by two, from 159 to 157. This is equal to the change in cash on the cash flow statement in the same year in Table 1.6. Earnings on cash and securities appear on the income statement in Table 1.5, and are assumed to be 1 percent of the balance in the previous year. Along with operating profits and interest expenses, the firm makes pretax earnings of 177 and pays taxes of 53, resulting in a net income of 124 in Year 3. These earnings and taxes are also reflected in the cash flow from operating activities on the cash flow statement, and are part of the firm's financial resources for investments.

The specification of the previous year's balance, not the same year's, for earnings on cash and securities is to avoid circulation in calculation. In circulation, net income depends on earnings on cash and securities, which depend on changes in cash flow, which depends on net income, and so on. Such circulation is made possible by running the iteration function in Excel, which determines each value simultaneously, but the model is kept simple without it.

Reflecting these earnings and distribution, the net assets of the firm increase by 24 from 1,332 to 1,356, the result of the addition of the net income of 124 in Year 3 and the share repurchase of 100. Although the amount of share repurchase is constant in this model, a firm may adjust the level according to the cash flow it has available for distribution to investors. This is different from dividend payments, which investors expect to be constant or increasing once initiated.

The use of a share repurchase as an adjustment of cash flow indicates that the item is a **plug** for the purpose of financial modeling. Since a balance sheet needs to balance, it always needs a plug to fill in the gap that remains after all the other cash inflows and outflows are accounted for with operating, investment, and financing activities. The choice of a share issuance or repurchase as a plug means that the firm pays out cash to shareholders when it is redundant, but issues additional shares at times of cash deficiency. Models can use other items as plugs, such as cash or debt. For instance, if a firm decides to accumulate cash in preparation for contingencies rather than distributing it to investors, its cash balance increases, and it can spend part of this amount should it experience a cash deficiency. Similarly, if a firm decides to prepay debt instead of repurchasing shares, its debt balance falls accordingly, and when it faces cash deficiency it fills in the gap by borrowing. In reality, firms deploy a combination of these measures according to their liquidity needs, debt level, and payout policy.

6.3. Free cash flow

The financial model allows us to calculate free cash flow from the firm's financial statements. For instance, the firm's net operating profit after tax (NOPAT) in Year 3 is $195 \times (1 - 30\%) = 136$, as shown in Table 1.6.

By adding back the depreciation and amortization of 154 and subtracting the capital expenditure of 169 and the increase in net working capital of 10, the free cash flow is $(136 + 154 - 169 - 10) = 111$, which is consistent with the original projection shown in Table 1.2.

We can also calculate free cash flow by using the cash flow statement in Table 1.6. The difference between the cash flow from operating activities and the cash flow from investing activities, which is $(267 - 169) = 98$, gives a good approximation. The difference from 111 arises from the fact that the cash flow from operating activities does reflect interest expenses and earnings on cash and securities, which are respectively 20 and 2 in Year 3 on the income statement. The amount of tax is also affected by these expenses and earnings. Since these are irrelevant to the value of the firm's intrinsic operations, they are removed in calculating free cash flow. By restoring the after-tax interest expenses, which are $20 \times (1 - 30\%) = 14$, and subtracting the after-tax earnings on cash and securities, which are $2 \times (1 - 30\%) = 1$, we are able to reconcile the difference and reach the same value, which is $(98 + 14 - 1) = 111$.

Among all of a firm's financial statements, it is its operating earnings appearing on the income statement that are key to its free cash flow. This is why the operating margin is an important value driver in evaluating a firm's ability to generate free cash flow. The margin also relates to return on invested capital, which measures the effectiveness of a firm's investments.

6.4. Summary

Finally, let us summarize by looking over the structure of the financial model. The model captures the financial aspects of a firm's activities, mainly from the investment and financing perspectives. While a model is different from reality, it enables us to see the future of a firm and value it in the present, with a solid understanding of what drives it. A firm's activities are often described in accounting terms. A financial model that connects financial statements is helpful in bridging accounting and finance, and also in checking the consistency of projections, because, as we have noted, a balance sheet needs to balance.

As one means of ensuring consistency, note that all changes on the balance sheet are reflected in the cash flow statement. To reiterate, for the investment section, net change in fixed assets on the balance sheet is reflected as gross depreciation and amortization as well as capital expenditure on the cash flow statement. Similarly, gross changes in accounts receivable, inventory, and accounts payable on the balance sheet are reflected as changes in net working capital on the cash flow statement. And for the financing section, change in net assets on the balance sheet is reflected on the cash flow statement as pretax earnings and taxes as well as share issuance or repurchase. Change in debt balance on the balance sheet is reflected on the cash flow statement as borrowing or repayment of debt. Finally, the residual of all these changes is the change in cash on the balance sheet, which is also reflected as change in cash on the cash flow statement.

The financial model converts these results into free cash flow, a concise indicator of a firm's performance. Free cash flow is the fundamental variable of firm value. It indicates the effectiveness of a firm's investments and its underlying strategy, thereby enabling it to continue to finance its investments in the financial markets.

7. Conclusion

While the term "value" can refer to several aspects of our personal or societal values, financial value is the foremost concept in the context of financial management. This is because a firm requires financial resources to initiate, grow, and sustain its business. To manage value well we need to understand it well. The goal of financing is to secure capital in the financial markets for a firm's investments before they generate value. This involves uncertainty on the side of the investors who provide such capital, for which they demand a risk premium. When a firm succeeds through its strategies in securing capital and generating value, investors are rewarded with a financial return which enables them to reinvest in new investment opportunities.

The exchange of capital under conditions of uncertainty requires us to assess the prospects of a firm's value creation and its own degree of uncertainty. Free cash flow expresses the scale of the value that a firm creates and makes available for distribution to its investors. A firm's projections also offer information on the timing of free cash flow. The degree of uncertainty is measured by a required rate of return that reflects risk. A model to derive such a return must be based on a general understanding of the state of the overall market and a specific understanding of the investee firm. The CAPM offers a simple but consistent model for this purpose, as it positions a firm's relative risk in the overall market and adjusts its required return accordingly.

A firm's major source of value — projected free cash flow — can be understood with financial modeling. A financial model helps us make informed decision on investments by enabling us to understand the key value drivers of firms and their sensitivity to value. Although assessing the future inherently carries uncertainty, a financial model helps us see into the future by incorporating key drivers and their impact on value. Framing a firm in such a model requires a knowledge of financial statements and their interrelationships in converting accounting expressions into financial value. These financial methodologies enable us to assess and understand the effectiveness of a firm's investments and its underlying strategy in a context of uncertainty.

Chapter 2

Making Capital Investment Decisions

I. Overview

Building on the concept of value developed in the previous chapter, we now discuss the decision rules on which firms base their **capital investments**. From the viewpoint of investors, a firm's raison d'être lies in its ability to do what they cannot: explore, select, and undertake investment projects. When investors find a firm with a comparative advantage, they delegate such decisions to its managers while contributing the capital needed for such projects.

As with definitions of value, decision rules can be set in diverse ways that depend on their objective. In the realm of financial management, value means financial value, and maximizing value is the objective of capital investment decisions. It may not be the sole, firm-wide objective, since a firm deals with other kinds of value as well, including customer satisfaction, responsible sourcing, and employee wellness. But as long as a firm relies on capital from investors, the maximization of financial value is an indispensable element of its management.

Even when decision rules are based solely on maximizing financial value, they may not be straightforward. Such value can be further broken down into value which is certain or uncertain, or short-term or long-term, meaning that managers must compare value with different risks at different points in time. One thing that is helpful when converting between future and present value is a consideration of uncertainty, as this allows managers to discern truly value-creating projects from others.

There are various ways of making capital investments. A firm can invest in building a warehouse or online platform from scratch (a *greenfield* investment), or in purchasing an existing asset and even an entire firm (a *brown-field* investment). Investments in corporate equity are also an essential part of a firm's capital investments in that the acquired or investee firms go on to make their own capital investments in businesses; the original firm thus makes those capital investments indirectly via its investees.

In the following sections, we discuss the use of net present value (NPV) and internal rate of return (IRR) as main criteria for capital investment decisions. We then cover the application of the discounted cash flow (DCF) analysis developed in the previous chapter to investment in firms. In this context, we also consider the method of using comparables. We then look at economic profit and return on invested capital (ROIC), which are variations of the NPV and the internal rate of return, and relate them to valuation based on discounted cash flow. Finally, we discuss how investment decisions connect to a firm's capability-building and real options from the viewpoint of strategic management.

2. Decision Rules

2.1. *Investment in projects*

2.1.1. *Net Present Value*

The mainstream decision rule is based on the **NPV** of a project. NPV is the difference between the present value of a project's future free cash flow and the value of initial investment required at present. If the NPV of a project is positive, it means that a firm is expected to add value by undertaking the project. Adding value here does not mean that a firm creates value which is larger than zero, but that it creates an *excess* value relative to its required cost of capital. This is obvious from the calculation process for present value, which uses the opportunity cost of capital, a reflection of the return that could be obtained if the capital were deployed elsewhere.

In a similar example to one developed in the previous chapter, suppose that a project is expected to generate free cash flow of 111, in million dollars, in three years and that the required rate of return for the project is 7 percent in consideration of its risk and other investment opportunities.

Table 2.1 NPV and IRR.

Year		1	2	3
Discount rate	7%			
FCF — base case	−90	0	0	111
NPV	1			
IRR	7.2%			
FCF — downside case	−90	0	0	100
NPV	−8			
IRR	3.6%			
FCF — upside case	−90	0	0	120
NPV	8			
IRR	10.1%			

A summary of three scenarios — base, downside, and upside — is shown in Table 2.1. Assume additionally that the project requires an initial investment of 90. Since the present value of free cash flow from the project is $111/1.07^3 = 91$, the NPV of this project is $(91 - 90) = 1$. Undertaking this project, therefore, means that the firm adds value by one million dollars.

After three years, suppose in the base case that the project turns out to be a success, generating the exact amount of the expected free cash flow. This means that the firm realizes net profits of $(111 - 90) = 21$. But because the firm could earn similar profits from other projects, its earnings barely exceed the break-even point in terms of the opportunity cost of capital. From an investor's viewpoint, too, it is a fair return in that similar returns could be earned by investing capital in other firms.

Next, suppose instead in the downside case that the firm generates free cash flow of only 100 after three years, short of the original projection of 111. In this case, even though the firm still earns net profits of $(100 - 90) = 10$, it is seen as a *loss* in economic terms in that the earnings level is below the opportunity cost of capital. In a backward calculation, earning 100 would have meant a negative NPV of $(100/1.07^3 - 90) = -8$ at the time of decision. Hence, it is seen as a value-destroying proposition.

In contrast, if the firm does better than expected in the upside case and generates free cash flow of 120, it means that it generates excess profit well above the opportunity cost of capital. In this case, the NPV would have been $(120/1.07^3 - 90) = 8$ at the time of decision. This is true value creation in economic terms, as it exceeds the opportunity cost of capital. Here, we see that success or failure is determined based on the opportunity cost of capital that a firm must deal with in undertaking a project.

2.1.2. Internal Rate of Return

A similar argument can be made by using a project's **Internal Rate of Return (IRR)**. IRR is a compound rate of return that makes the NPV of a project equal zero given a free cash flow projection. For instance, the same project with a free cash flow of 111 in the base case, on the initial investment of 90, earns an internal rate of return of $(111/90)^{1/3} - 1 = 7.2$ percent over the three years. This means that the investment earns a rate of return of 7.2 percent annually on the investment, as $90 \times 1.072^3 = 111$. To confirm the calculation, the NPV of the project with a discount rate of 7.2 percent is zero, or $(111/1.072^3) - 90 = 0$. The result of 7.2 percent is slightly above the required rate of return of 7 percent. This is similar to the result for net present value, which is also slightly above the threshold of zero.

Likewise, if the project generates free cash flow of only 100 in the downside case, its IRR is $(100/90)^{1/3} - 1 = 3.6$ percent, well below the required rate of 7 percent. In contrast, if it generates free cash flow of 120 in the upside case, the rate is $(120/90)^{1/3} - 1 = 10.1$ percent, well exceeding the required rate. In this way, IRR can be used in relation to a required rate of return, which is essentially a **hurdle rate** for a project's internal approval.

In practice, the IRR for a project that generates free cash flow over multiple years is calculated by applying the IRR function of Excel to a cash flow projection which includes initial investment, a negative cash flow. The function calculates IRR through an iterative process, as it is hard to solve a multi-dimensional equation otherwise. In contrast, there is no Excel function which directly calculates NPV, because the NPV function, unlike the IRR function, deals only with cash flows starting on and after a year from the present, and thereby excludes initial investments made at the outset. For this reason, one needs to apply the NPV function to obtain the *gross* present value of future cash flows and subtract the amount of initial investment from the output for the *net* present value.

While both NPV and IRR are used in practice, an NPV-based rule has some advantages over the other. NPV is additive, for instance, while IRR is not. If a firm executes a project with an NPV of 10 and another with one of 20, the total is 30. IRR does not have such additivity. NPV has an additional advantage in that it allows one to measure the absolute size of value created. IRR does not indicate such size, so a small investment with a high IRR may actually generate just a small amount of money. Instead, IRR is superior in indicating relative return, as it allows one to measure the efficiency of capital deployed in comparison with a hurdle rate set internally. NPV can also be applied to projections in general, while IRR requires care in one exceptional case: When free cash flow changes over the term of a project from negative to positive, and again to negative, and so on, equations for IRR can confuse managers by having multiple solutions.

In practice, both NPV and IRR are widely used in a complementary manner, because the latter still has its own advantages despite a few drawbacks. This is also consistent with the general method of measuring value both in dollar amounts and rates of return.

2.2. Investment in firms

2.2.1. DCF in capital investment and M&A

While NPV and IRR are applied to green-field capital investments, such as building physical stores or expanding online outlets, the same concepts are applied in evaluating whole firms as well, such as when a firm acquires a retailer or invests in an online startup. The performance of firm-wide investments is evaluated using the same logic as that for matters involving the efficiency of capital deployed. The two methods assess individual projects, but also assess firms generating cash flow as a whole. As the costs of capital investment projects are borne by firms, it is unsurprising to see capital investment projects take the form of investment in firms already undertaking such projects or planning to do so.

When applying the NPV rule to firm-wide investment as a decision rule, we compare the investment value, which is the market price of a firm in public markets or a negotiated one, against a value based on the discounted cash flow. The latter value is the present value of a future exit price and payouts during the investment period. Investment in firms at a current price that is less than its calculated value is expected to add value, and vice versa. Similarly, an internal rate of return is obtained from the initial investment price, payouts during the investment period, and the exit price.

In addition, firms deciding to acquire other firms often have indefinite investment horizons. A firm may invest in another that already has investment projects underway, in a firm-wide capital investment. This is the practice known as **mergers and acquisitions**, which we shall discuss in Chapter 5. The basic economics behind such decisions is the same as for in-house capital investments; therefore, the decision rules are no different from those applied to the latter.

We should note, however, that the synergetic effects of mergers and acquisitions are explicitly taken into account. **Synergy** is the difference between the value of a combined business and the total value of separate businesses. It represents excess economic profits that a firm can only realize through a business combination, and which investors cannot replicate simply by investing in separate firms. Excess profits are also gained by undertaking in-house capital investment projects. A firm does this because it believes these projects will generate profits that its competitors will not be able to match, given comparative advantages such as customer platform, employees skills, and brand equity. Any excess profits generated by such capital investments are implicitly included in projected cash flows. They may not be referred to as synergy, but their economic sense is the same.

In estimating synergy in the context of mergers and acquisitions, the free cash flow projections in a financial model are revised upward to reflect the expected value added. The incremental free cash flow of a combined firm is a major source of synergy, appearing either as greater inflow in the form of increased revenues, or less outflow in the form of reduced costs. The risk of the new firm may also change after such a firm-wide investment, to be reflected accordingly in the firm's required rate of return. It may be more dominant and stable, requiring a lower rate, or may be riskier in its new composition, requiring a higher rate. The decision rule is to compare the negotiated price of acquisition against the fundamental value including the synergy, both in present-value terms. If the former is lower than the latter, the acquirer is likely to add value through the transaction. However, if the planned synergy fails to emerge, it means the acquirer has paid more than it actually recoups, and ends up losing value.

2.2.2. Comparable

The **comparable** method is a means of quickly valuating a firm based on a comparison of the multiples of the firm's value to certain metrics, such as earnings, with those of its competitors, or "comparable" firms. Such firms are comparable in terms of the business and market risks to which they are exposed, although strategies and market positions may differ. The data on these multiples are publicly available for listed firms. As it provides a relative valuation, the comparable method is used along with the DCF method as a reality check for valuation results.

Major multiples referred to in practice are the multiple of equity value to earnings, or **price-to-earnings ratio (PER)**, and the multiple of firm value to earnings before interest, taxes, depreciation, and amortization (EBITDA). The **EBITDA multiple** has the advantage of not being affected by the degree of leverage, which is a drawback of the PER. Its numerator is the value of a whole firm and its denominator is earnings before paying interest, meaning that neither is affected by the level of debt. Also, it indicates earnings before expensing depreciation and amortization, which are regularly added back to derive free cash flow. EBITDA is an effective metric for capital-intensive industries where the amount of depreciation and amortization can be large relative to earnings. A different version is the multiple of firm value to operating earnings, or earnings before interest and taxes (EBIT). The **EBIT multiple** is suited to firms with relatively little investment in depreciable, tangible assets.

In contrast to free cash flow, neither EBITDA nor EBIT reflect investment activities. Rather, they look at the earning power of a firm's asset base as a result of past investment activities, and the financial leeway it has to invest without resorting to external financing. Nor do they reflect taxes, which differ across tax jurisdictions. Since the actual value delivered to investors is after taxes, an apparent difference in multiples may be due to differences in the tax treatment of firms operating in different jurisdictions.

The comparable method is widely used in valuing startups as well. Startups typically face a cash deficiency in their early stages of growth and continue to burn cash while financing projects. Some, failing to get traction with their intended goods or services, may overshoot the runway without taking off; others may transform themselves into big enterprises. Since it does not make sense to seek meaningful cash flow projections for firms at such an early stage, it is useful to resort to relative valuation by examining comparable firms for clues.

Let us consider an example. Suppose that a medical startup is seeking investment to develop an app which will track the health of users and offer tailor-made medical advice based on the accumulated data. It attracts users of all ages, and its beta version already has two million people registered. But because these are not paid users, it has not generated a positive cash flow, and its investment in developing and marketing the app exceeds its advertising revenues.

A competitor firm targets children and their parents by offering an app to monitor the children's physical and mental state, including free games suitable for each age. It, too, has generated no meaningful non-advertising revenue, although it expects to monetize its user base by charging for additional monitoring and gaming functions. It recently succeeded in obtaining Series B funding at a valuation of $1.2 billion for six million registered users.

In this scenario, the number of registered users is a key metric, since both firms run cash deficits by continuously investing in developing and marketing their apps. Investors in the latter firm value its users at $1.2 billion/6 million = $200 each on average, taking into account the value of accumulated data and expected revenues from future paid services and targeted advertisements. Applying the same logic and price, the medical startup is valued at 2 million × $200 = $0.4 billion. Alternatively, its value is simply a third of its competitor's, in proportion to the number of registered users.

Institutional investors such as venture capital funds assess growth potential before investing in a startup. They exit an investment by selling their holdings to firms that want to invest in the field or by listing the shares on the stock exchange. Large firms often engage in **corporate venture capital (CVC)** to invest in startups, which offers their investee companies resources for growth. For such firms, evaluating startups with unpredictable cash flows is an integral part of their capital investment activities.

In predicting free cash flow, a high level of uncertainty does not mean there are no clues at all to assist in making investment decisions. In place of free cash flow, various other metrics are examined, such as the volume of customer traffic, growth rate of the market by segment, amount of investment required, speed of operating margin improvement, and timing of turning from loss to profitability. These are a firm's key value drivers which ultimately lead to a positive free cash flow. Assessment of the management team is generally what matters most in valuing a startup, but these other metrics are valuable in that they contribute to generating a positive cash flow in the future. As is the case with free cash flow projections, projections of these key value drivers typically require a **scenario analysis**, a type of sensitivity analysis that examines divergent possible outcomes and metrics in play at one time, depending on market conditions and competition, including outright failure. By analyzing possible scenarios and their impact on these metrics, one can assess the risks and opportunities of potential investments.

3. Performance Evaluations

After an investment is decided upon and executed, its performance is evaluated based on subsequent value added, by looking at such factors as growth in earnings, free cash flow, and market value. The basis for these evaluations is a comparison of original cash flow projections with actual results. Some measures of capital efficiency are also deployed, such as **return on assets (ROA)**, **return on equity (ROE)**, and **return on invested capital (ROIC)**. The performance of equity investments in public markets is measured by **total shareholder return (TSR)**, which is the sum of capital gains and dividends divided by the purchase price of stock. TSR can also be used to measure annual stock performance by replacing the initial investment price with the beginning-of-year share price. These performance metrics are monitored and evaluated against their original investment theses, and are typically tied to the compensation paid to managers.

3.1. Economic profit

It is relatively easy to assess financial performance at the firm level, as financial statements and stock prices are available on a firm-wide basis. However, capital investment projects conducted within a firm lack such information, unless they are structured and operated as if they were separate firms. In this case, performance evaluation requires **managerial accounting** based on internal information on specific projects or the divisions in charge of such projects.

One way to perform such an internal evaluation is to look at the earnings attributed to projects or divisions by allocating revenues and costs internally according to business. Firm-wide costs, too, are often allocated by applying internally defined cost drivers, such as hours spent for specific divisions, to examine divisional performance analogous to firm-wide performance.

However, managerial accounting measures often fail to consider required cost of capital, which is based on economic opportunity cost. Not accounting for the cost of the capital deployed for a project may give managers an undesirable incentive to negotiate for the maximum capital budget possible in order to maximize their divisional earnings. It would also be illogical if divisional managers were not evaluated relative to a required cost of capital while the whole firm was evaluated on that basis in the financial markets. For this reason, **economic profit** measures the performance of projects or divisions by subtracting the corresponding cost of capital from the profits they earn. Economic profit is similar to NPV in that it reflects the cost of capital in obtaining value, but the former is typically used for periodical assessments after decisions are made, while the latter is used prior to decisions and as a lump sum at the outset.

The idea of economic profit originated with Alfred Marshall in the 19th century.[1] It was commercialized as an analytical tool in the 1980s under the trademark of Economic Value Added (EVA), which is now run by Institutional Shareholder Services, a proxy advisory firm.

Specifically, economic profit is calculated as follows:

$$EP = EBIT(1-t) - IC \times r_{WACC}$$

where EP is the economic profit, $EBIT$ is earnings before interest and taxes, t is corporate tax rate, IC is invested capital, and r_{WACC} is the weighted average cost of capital (WACC). EBIT is a project-based metric or divisional metric based on managerial accounting for evaluation. Similarly based on managerial accounting is **invested capital**, which is the sum of the book value of the equity capital and the debt capital allocated to specific businesses. Debt capital is often limited to that which is long-term and interest-bearing. The WACC applied to the invested capital for projects or divisions may be the same as a firm-wide WACC, but if a firm runs multiple businesses with very different risk profiles, the WACC is tailored to the risk level; managers would otherwise be undesirably incentivized to adopt high-risk projects while rejecting low-risk ones

---

[1] Marshall, A. (1890). *Principles of Economics*. London, UK: MacMillan & Co.

relative to the firm's average cost of capital, thus destroying value by undertaking undesirable projects while passing on desirable ones. This caution also applies to evaluations based on NPV and IRR that apply a cost of capital.

A useful feature of economic profit is its direct linkage to firm value calculated from discounted cash flow. It is shown that the market value of a firm's equity is equal to the sum of the present value of its economic profits over the years and the book value of its equity. That is:

$$V_E = B_E + \sum_{t=1}^{\infty} \frac{EP_t}{(1+r)^t}$$

where V_E is the market value of a firm's equity, B_E is the book value, EP_t is the economic profit for the period of t, and r is the discount rate, which is the required rate of return for the risk entailed in the economic profit.[2] This means that the economic profit is the value *in excess of* the book value of equity, something not accounted for on the balance sheet. This is also the foundation for the **price-to-book ratio (PBR)**, which is the ratio of the market value of equity over its book value.

The relationship between firm value and economic profit is similar, since firm value is the sum of equity value and debt value. Adding the book value of debt to both sides of the equation, by approximating its market value by its book value, shows that the economic profit is the value in excess of the book value of a whole firm.

Let us look at an example in Table 2.2. Suppose that a firm's net operating profit after tax (NOPAT) is constant at 100, in million dollars. This is equal to $EBIT\,(1-t)$. The firm has invested capital, or an asset, of 1,000 at the outset, and makes no additional investment. The asset is depreciated and amortized in five years by 200 a year. Its free cash flow

---

[2]Here is a proof: Where B_t is the book value of net assets at the end of period t, I_t is net income for the period of t, and C_t is cash flow distributed to shareholders, $E_t = E_{t-1} + I_t - C_t$. Where r is the cost of capital and R_t is the economic profit, $R_t = I_t - rE_{t-1}$ by definition. Therefore, $C_t = E_{t-1} + I_t - E_t = R_t + (1+r)E_{t-1} - E_t$. The equity value, V_E, is the sum of the cash flow C_t discounted by r. When $t = 1$, the present value of C_1 is $R_1/(1+r) + E_0 - E_1/(1+r)$, and when $t = 2$, the present value of C_2 is $R_2/(1+r)^2 + E_1/(1+r) - E_2/(1+r)^2$, and so on. When summing up all of the equations, all terms after $t = 1$ that include E_t are offset against each other, leaving $V_E = \Sigma\,(C_t) = \Sigma\,(R_t) + E_0$.

Table 2.2   Economic profit.

Year		1	2	3	4	5
1	EBIT $(1-t)$	100	100	100	100	100
2	Invested capital	1,000	800	600	400	200
3	Depreciation	200	200	200	200	200
4	FCF $(1+3)$	300	300	300	300	300
5	Present value (4×13)	280	262	245	229	214
6	PV of FCF	1,230				
7	EP $(1-2 \times 12)$	30	44	58	72	86
8	Present value (7×13)	28	38	47	55	61
9	PV of EP	230				
10	Value of IC	1,000				
11	Sum $(9+10)$	1,230				
12	Discount rate	7%				
13	Discount factor	0.93	0.87	0.82	0.76	0.71

is then $(100 + 200) = 300$, and the sum of the present value of the free cash flows for five years is 1,230 with a discount rate of 7 percent.

Under the same assumptions, the economic profit of the firm in Year 1 is $(100 - 1,000 \times 7\%) = 30$. Since the asset is depreciated and amortized by 200, the invested capital decreases to 800 in Year 2. Reflecting this, the economic profit in Year 2 improves to $(100 - 800 \times 7\%) = 44$. We calculate the economic profits similarly for the following years. The sum of the present value of the economic profits for five years is 230. Adding the initial invested capital of 1,000, we reach the same value of $(230 + 1,000) = 1,230$.

In this way, we are able to connect economic profit to firm value. This relationship is useful along with managerial accounting for managing not only entire firms but their internal divisions. While it may be difficult for divisional managers to maximize the value of an entire firm, it is relatively easy, and practical, for them to maximize the economic profits of divisions under their direct control. For this reason, economic profit is an effective way to manage financial value within a firm by taking required cost of capital into account.

However, internally charging the cost of invested capital annually calls for due care in regard to an investment's long-term contribution.

Since a capital charge increases with the level of invested capital, managers have an incentive to restrain investments so that invested capital remains low, resulting in higher economic profit. While the objective of economic profit is to make visible the economic cost of capital owed by a firm to its investors, it can give managers an adverse incentive to pass on investment opportunities that would be desirable for the firm in the long term but undesirable for their own evaluations in the short term. This requires a sort of balancing act when evaluating managers at the divisional and even the firm-wide level, to ensure that capital investments contributing to long-term firm value are encouraged, while overinvestment in search of short-term earnings is not.

3.2. Return on invested capital

The formula for economic profit can be converted as follows by dividing both sides of the equation by invested capital (IC):

$$EP/IC = EBIT(1-t)/IC - r_{WACC}$$

The ratio of $EBIT$ $(1-t)$ to IC on the right-hand side is called **return on invested capital (ROIC)**. This measures the efficiency of capital invested in businesses. With the definition of ROIC, we then obtain the following equation:

$$EP = (ROIC - r_{WACC}) \times IC$$

This equation shows that the economic profit represents the *excess* earning power of invested capital measured by ROIC over the cost of capital, or WACC, that a firm faces in the financial markets.

From the definition of ROIC, it follows:

$$ROIC = EBIT(1-t)/Sales \times Sales/IC$$

The equation indicates that the sources of high ROIC are a high operating margin, expressed by the first term on the right hand, and a high turnover of capital, expressed by the second term. There is a trade-off between the two: While a firm needs to continuously invest capital to sustain a margin, expansion of invested capital restrains the capital turnover. Because the premise of economic profit is that a firm's excess earnings level is sustained into the future, this again shows the importance of appropriately evaluating the effects of long-term capital investments.

The level of ROIC also relates to a firm's payout policy. If shareholders enjoy an excess return by virtue of a firm's competitive advantage, they are better off letting the firm retain its earnings rather than distributing them. For example, suppose that a firm continues to generate an ROIC of 10 percent against its WACC of 7 percent. Its payout ratio, which is the amount of dividends and repurchases over earnings, is 40 percent. The firm reinvests all of the retained earnings in capital investment, which generates the same return. Table 2.3 shows the results.

From Year 1 to 2, as a result of retaining 60 out of the earnings of 100, in million dollars, the invested capital of the firm increases 6 percent from 1,000 to 1,060. Since the increased capital generates the same rate of return, earnings in Year 2 increase by the same rate from 100 to 106. This leads to a 6 percent increase in the amounts of both payouts and retained earnings in Year 2. This then increases the invested capital by another 6 percent, from 1,060 in Year 2 to 1,124 in Year 3. In this way, the invested capital, earnings, payouts, and retained earnings all grow at the same rate. This occurs without external financing for growth, as it is financed solely with retained earnings. The growth rate, 6 percent in this example, is the **sustainable growth rate**. It depends on the return on invested capital and the payout ratio, expressed as follows:

$$Sustainable\,growth\,rate = ROIC \times (1 - payout\,ratio)$$

Table 2.3   Sustainable growth rate.

Year		1	2	3	4	5
1	Invested capital (IC)	1,000	1,060	1,124	1,191	1,262
2	Earnings (1×5)	100	106	112	119	126
3	Payouts (2×7)	40	42	45	48	50
4	Retained earnings ($2 - 3$)	60	64	67	71	76
5	ROIC	10%				
6	WACC	7%				
7	Payout ratio	40%				
8	Growth rate ($5 \times (100\% - 7)$)	6%				

We can confirm with the formula that the sustainable growth rate of the firm is $10\% \times (1 - 40\%) = 6\%$, exactly the rate at which the firm grows its invested capital, earnings, payouts, and retained earnings each year.

The equation shows that a combination of a high (low) ROIC and a low (high) payout ratio corresponds to a high (low) growth rate. Hence, it is not a coincidence that a growth firm retains most of its earnings for expansion and often resorts to external financing for additional capital, whereas a mature firm does the opposite, paying out most of its earnings and even shedding some of its stagnant businesses for additional payouts.

It is hard work for a firm to sustain profitability while continuing to grow at a constant rate. In reality, there is often a tradeoff between ROIC and growth rate. Deviation from the sustainable growth rate formula is larger when a firm does not finance itself, but resorts to the financial markets for additional financing and distribution. An expanding product market requires a high level of capital investment and attracts new entrants, resulting in a growing market with a low ROIC. When a firm finances its expansion with additional external financing, its ROIC becomes even lower than its supposed sustainable growth rate, by making its denominator larger. In contrast, a mature, low-growth product market requires little capital investment and induces exits, leading to a high ROIC for surviving players despite the stagnancy of the market. ROIC becomes even higher when a firm curbs its investments and distributes the capital to external investors, making the denominator smaller.

This corresponds to the "star"/"cash cow" contrast in **product portfolio management (PPM)**[3]: A star product or business requires a high level of investment to sustain its leadership position in a growing market; thus, its free cash flow tends to be negative, requiring external financing. A cash cow's investment requirements plateau in a maturing market, and the business generates excess free cash flow by virtue of a strong market position, which is internally allocated to the star to fund its fast growth.

3.3. *IRR*

Finally, performance is also evaluated by means of the internal rate of return (IRR). IRR is a function of value and time, and a high (low) value

---

[3]Henderson, B. (1970). The product portfolio. *Perspectives, 66.* Boston Consulting Group.

Table 2.4   IRR, multiples and time.

	1x	2x	3x	4x	5x	6x	7x	8x	9x	10x
1	0%	100%	200%	300%	400%	500%	600%	700%	800%	900%
2	0%	41%	73%	100%	124%	145%	165%	183%	200%	216%
3	0%	26%	44%	59%	71%	82%	91%	100%	108%	115%
4	0%	19%	32%	41%	50%	57%	63%	68%	73%	78%
5	0%	15%	25%	32%	38%	43%	48%	52%	55%	58%
6	0%	12%	20%	26%	31%	35%	38%	41%	44%	47%
7	0%	10%	17%	22%	26%	29%	32%	35%	37%	39%
8	0%	9%	15%	19%	22%	25%	28%	30%	32%	33%
9	0%	8%	13%	17%	20%	22%	24%	26%	28%	29%
10	0%	7%	12%	15%	17%	20%	21%	23%	25%	26%

added in a short (long) period of time results in a high (low) IRR. Table 2.4 shows this relationship, with multiples of the value of investment over its initial value on the horizontal axis, and years required to realize them on the vertical axis. The shaded area shows where IRR is higher than a threshold of 30 percent.

The matrix shows that the longer it takes to raise value, the higher is the multiple required to meet a threshold. For instance, an IRR exceeding 30 percent is achievable with the value of four times ("4x") its original investment if five years are required, in which case the IRR is 32 percent. The hurdle rises, however, if it takes longer: When ten years are required, even a 10-times valuation results in a rate of return which is short of the threshold at 26 percent. The table summarizes the short-term thinking of some investment funds, which aim for a high rate of return by achieving a target value quickly. Taking a long-term view requires correspondingly high value to meet an expected return.

In evaluating the performance of venture capital and private equity fund investments, the multiple is regularly used to measure value added for individual investee firms. The ratio of the equity value at the time of exit to that at the time of investment is called the **multiple on invested capital (MOIC)**. This indicates a gross value added independent of time horizon, which is then translated into an IRR by reflecting the time needed to achieve it. To realize an expected return, fund managers see how investee firms' margin, growth, capital efficiency, and other milestone value drivers compare with those of their peers along specific time horizons.

4. Capability Building

The previous two sections showed how we measure the financial performance of a firm through free cash flow, net present value, internal rate of return, economic profit, and return on invested capital. These metrics guide managers in their strategic decisions. Reflecting the interrelationship among strategic decisions, value drivers, and financial performance, the role of managers increasingly includes dealing with a firm's strategic and financial aspects simultaneously.

Decisions on mergers and acquisitions are integrative in nature, in that they require the valuation of a target firm and an assessment of a decision's impact on the existing firm in both strategic and financial terms. Managers reassess possible changes in their firm's market position, and metrics that relate to its future financial performance, while negotiating the terms and structures of a deal. These analyses are also used when communicating with shareholders, whose approval may be required under some structures. Similarly, decisions on in-house capital investment projects call for an assessment of their incremental impact on the firm's businesses and markets as well as financials such as earnings and margins. Even after a decision is made, the performance resulting from their actions is periodically reported to investors and is reflected in the firm's stock price. These communications require direct knowledge of strategic and financial decisions.

Managers, in particular financial managers, are also expected to identify gaps in evaluation between themselves and investors and propose ideas for ways to fill them in, such as by entering into new segments, executing mergers and acquisitions, or exiting from unpromising businesses. Financial managers are closer to investors than others within a firm and are positioned to link a firm to the financial markets. Thus, they are in the best position to explore value-enhancing opportunities, by dealing proactively with areas that investors feel are lacking and by managing perceptions in the financial markets.

Such actions are a departure from the otherwise passive role of financial managers, who spend most of their time preparing and disclosing financial statements and securing operating funds. Financial managers are increasingly required to take an integrative view of their firm, from outside as well as inside the organization, while communicating with the financial markets and working to enhance their company's value in them. It is not surprising, then, that a significant portion of the CEOs of the U.S. Fortune 500 and S&P 500 companies come directly from CFO positions in major sectors: 25.5 percent in the financial sector, 19.6 percent in the consumer sector, and 13.7 percent in the services and industrial sectors.[4]

4.1. Firm capabilities

Given the interconnectedness of strategy and finance, capital investment decisions need to consider the building of sources of value, or **capability**, within a firm. Value sources include establishing a competitive market position and brand equity as bases for holistic, long-term growth, as opposed to simply crunching numbers in financial projections in an effort to arrive at agreeable margins and costs for specific projects. This broader view implies that executing a project is, essentially, building a firm's unique capabilities, where we can regard a firm as a bundle of projects with internal connections. A project affects a firm's contour, since a failed project harms the brand equity of the whole firm while a successful one enhances or even redefines it. A case in point is Pfizer, whose successful vaccine rollout during the pandemic led it to expand into the new gene-based technology behind its vaccine.[5]

Firms also need to adapt to changes in markets, sometimes by transforming themselves. They do this by building resources, or capabilities, which are responsive to the market environment. From this perspective, capital investments are often viewed as efforts to build **dynamic capabilities**, which are key assets of firms that survive in a changing business environment.[6] The need for such capabilities is not limited to fast-changing industries such as high-tech, but extends to many other areas that undergo change in markets and players over time.

There is an important distinction between static and dynamic capabilities. The former enable a firm to operate in ordinary circumstances; these

---

[4]Crist | Kolder Associates (2021). Volatility report 2021.
[5]Hopkins, J. S. (2021). Pfizer goes it alone to expand vaccine business beyond COVID-19 pandemic. *Wall Street Journal*, online edition, March 23, 2021.
[6]Teece, D. J., Pisano, G., and Shuen, A. (1997). Dynamic capabilities and strategic management. *Strategic Management Journal*, 18(7), 509–533.

are called "ordinary capabilities" for clarity.[7] The latter equip a firm with the readiness to make changes in the course of business. Such capabilities are dynamic in the literal sense, in that they emphasize a firm's ability to survive through continuous adaptation to its environment.

A key portion of such capabilities consists of investments in **intangible assets**. The Unilever brand, for instance, has been respected for a long time, but its message has evolved over the years. Sensing the shifting tastes and concerns of consumers, who have now attached equal importance to environmental issues and responsibilities as to the reliable performance of constituent chemicals, the company has adapted its campaigns and brand strategies in response. Similarly, Apple maintains its brand value with continued investment in marketing and advertising campaigns that distinguish the firm in response to challenges by competitors. Brand perception is dynamic rather than constant, reflecting competition and the evolving preferences of the market. As companies work to adapt to such changes, their choice of investments lets the position of their brand shift to protect their value.

In the same vein, investments in research and development form dynamic capabilities in the sense that the fruits of such activities can be developed in various directions once their costs are sunk. While R&D investment gives firms new growth trajectories, the knowledge gained from a research activity may find itself with nowhere to go. However, consider the case of Post-it, the 3M product which originated from the development of an easy-to-peel glue, an oxymoron for a glue, without any specific application in mind. Organizational insights into a firm's capabilities can turn an experiment into a successful product, rather than burying it in a stockpile of failures.

To succeed in these adaptive investments and responses, firms need to invest in people, for it is people who actually confront changes and propose ideas for transforming a business as opposed to adhering to established platforms. Indeed, investment in **human capital** is a major part of corporate investment decisions as it is central to a firm's capabilities and thus a foundation of its business. Investing in people through in-house training and learning programs produces employees with the broad

---

[7]Teece, D. J. (2014). The foundations of enterprise performance: Dynamic and ordinary capabilities in an (economic) theory of firms. *Academy of Management Perspectives*, 28(4), 328–352.

perspective needed to sense changes in markets and opportunities and the flexibility to deal with them.

4.2. Real options

There are costs involved in staying able to adapt, whether these take the form of brand investments or research and development. To some extent this is inevitable. Indeed, it would be highly profitable if an investment, once made, continued to generate handsome profits; but the reality is that firms need to make multiple investments in order to survive under different scenarios. Some projects prove to succeed as targeted in that they open up new avenues for growth, but others end in failure by producing no meaningful outcome. Overall, firms equip themselves to adapt to different market scenarios. From a financial perspective, this ability to adapt, while it may incur unnecessary costs in hindsight, is seen in firms' investing in **real options**.

Real options are the application of financial options, which are derivative products available in the financial markets, to real business settings. As firms invest in financial options to manage uncertainty in interest rates, exchange rates, or commodity prices, they also make capital investments to manage uncertainty in their real businesses and markets. These are also part of dynamic capabilities in which firms are willing to invest.

For instance, airlines often obtain options to purchase additional aircraft from suppliers such as Airbus and Boeing to ensure their ability to adjust capacity in terms of available seats and routes. Such options give them a right, but not an obligation, to purchase additional aircraft, which means that they can cancel purchases whenever there is a downturn but receive prioritized delivery whenever necessary. Similarly, firms may build warehouses larger than they initially need so that expansion will be less costly when growth in business requires larger space. These are *expansion options*.

Similarly, a firm may choose to pay a higher rent for the right to cancel its lease and be able to downsize at any time, rather than contracting for a fixed term and space for a lower rent or purchasing its own office building. A firm may also choose to build a small pilot plant before entering into full-fledged production, even if it knows that to do so will cost more than building a large plant at the outset. These are *exit options*.

In these cases, firms are investing extra capital to obtain flexibility in managing future uncertainty. As such uncertainty unfolds, it may turn out that they need no additional aircraft or office space, but do need more warehousing or production capacity. These outcomes show that some investments in these options may be unnecessary. Similarly, a brand investment may miss a targeted audience, and research and development may fail to capture a market's needs. However, without such investments a firm might be worse off in other possible scenarios by failing to adapt itself to actual developments. While it would be ideal if managers were able to foresee which investments will prove necessary, in reality they invest in options that give them the flexibility to deal with uncertainty. Such investments embody the capabilities that firms choose to build in order to be able to respond flexibly to potential changes.

Let us look at Figure 2.1 as an example. Suppose that a firm is considering investing in a risky project that costs 200, in million dollars, with divergent possible outcomes. In two years it realizes earnings of either 400, with a 40 percent probability, or 100, with a 60 percent probability. The NPV of this project is negative, calculated as $(0.4 \times 400 + 0.6 \times 100)/1.07^2 - 200 = -8$, assuming a cost of capital of 7 percent. Under the decision rule based on net present value, the firm's manager will reject this project.

However, suppose additionally that, after some efforts at improvement, the investment of 200 in this project can now be staged in two parts of 40 and 160, as shown in Figure 2.2. In this setting, the firm is able to invest 40 at present, and then wait to see the outcome. Only after learning more about the project's prospects does it need to decide whether to proceed with the project or abandon it. Reflecting the benefit of what is learned by the time of the second decision, the success rate of the investment is higher at 80 percent. The additional investment is conditional on

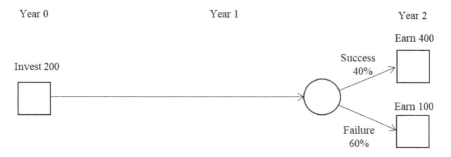

Figure 2.1 Investment without option.

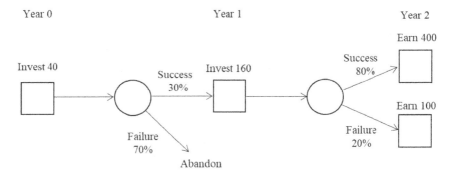

Figure 2.2 Investment with option.

the success of the first investment, which has a relatively low success rate of 30 percent.

To obtain the NPV in this setting, we need to calculate backward. First, the project's NPV in Year 1 is positive, calculated as $(0.8 \times 400 + 0.2 \times 100)/1.07 - 160 = 168$, based on the payoffs obtained in Year 2. Since the firm proceeds only when it finds the first investment successful, otherwise abandoning the entire project and cutting the loss of its initial investment of 40, the present value of the entire project is $(0.3 \times 168 + 0.7 \times 0)/1.07 - 40 = 4$, based on the payoffs obtained in Year 1. Since the value is positive, the firm proceeds with the initial investment.

In this case, by delaying a major part of its investment and waiting to learn more about the project before deciding whether to proceed, the firm invests in a real option which is valuable. The value of such an option is the difference in outcomes, which is $4 - (-8) = 12$. The firm is willing to pay for the option of delaying the investment until it has acquired greater knowledge. Such options may be created through the project's structuring, such as its setting of withdrawal rules and negotiating of contractual terms with other firms. In this way, uncertainty is mitigated by the firm's ability to obtain real options in its capital investment decisions. It also means that the firm has capabilities to deal with uncertainty.

These come with costs, however. Given that a firm is a risk-taking entity by nature, when facing uncertainty it must compare the benefits and the costs of keeping its options open. No firm can gain meaningful profits if it bets on every possible scenario; rather, it should be willing to take calculated risks by analyzing possible scenarios and discerning the types of risks it is well positioned to take, such as product development risk, from those it is not, such as commodity market risk. Since investors can easily diversify and hedge risk in their investments, the role of a firm conducting a capital investment project is to take and control desirable risks in a manner that investors cannot replicate. Identifying real options embedded in capital investment projects, and structuring and negotiating those projects so as to obtain them, is a clear example of a comparative advantage that a firm has over investors.

5. Conclusion

Firms with sound decision rules are able to make good decisions in that they know what they must do and are clear about the value and risks of the projects they undertake. Net present value, by which managers evaluate projects based on a projected free cash flow and a discount rate that reflects its risk, is the dominant rule that can be applied to any case. A complementary rule is the internal rate of return, which measures a project's profitability against a hurdle rate set internally by the firm. Firms may also use economic profit and return on invested capital, which place emphasis on excess profits over required rate of return in the financial markets.

Capital investments take various forms. In addition to such tangible assets as buildings and warehouses, firms invest in intangible assets such as brand, technology, and human capital. These investments can take the form of financial investments as well, such as the acquisition of stakes in firms, including startups, which undertake projects on their own. Mergers and acquisitions, which are investments in whole firms and combinations of businesses, are also a form of capital investment.

Decision rules for investment in firms are the same as those for investment in projects, in that the NPV of future cash flow, which reflects relevant risks, must be positive against the initial investment value. Mergers and acquisitions also require the combined value to be greater than the sum of the parts, otherwise called synergy. Synergy is something that only firms can achieve. Investors cannot obtain it simply by investing in separate firms.

Successful investments enable firms to build unique capabilities in competitive markets. Such capabilities are often dynamic, in that they enable firms to adapt to changes in their environment. In the financial realm, decisions taken to maintain such adaptability overlap with the purchase of real options. Together, these place firms in the position to handle uncertainty in the markets and thus to take calculated risks.

Because they are something that investors cannot do on their own, capital investments are firms' raison d'être. The ability of firms to explore, identify, and execute projects successfully enables them to survive, grow, and realize financial wealth for the investors that supply them with capital.

Chapter 3

Understanding Asymmetric Information in Financial Markets

1. Asymmetric Information

Financial markets are where firms and investors meet to exchange information and capital. Investors base their decisions on information they obtain from firms. But since investors exist outside a firm's boundaries, their information is inherently incomplete. Firms disclose information based on disclosure rules to which they are subject, but they do not disclose private information, such as proprietary know-how and customer information, which is kept within the firm. Therefore, there is always an information gap between firms and investors. This is what we call **asymmetric information**.

1.1. Adverse selection and moral hazard

Asymmetric information causes two types of problems: adverse selection and moral hazard.

Adverse selection arises when a better-informed party is unwilling to sell a high-quality item because it cannot obtain a fair price based on the information in its possession. Less-informed parties are aware of this, and, believing that the seller is more likely to offer low-quality items, have less of an incentive to buy. George Akerlof shows how adverse selection can be an undesirable result of buyers and sellers having asymmetric information on the quality of used cars.[1] Sellers, fearing that their cars may be undervalued by buyers having insufficient automotive information, are only willing to sell low-quality cars, or *lemons*, that truly deserve a low evaluation; they are unwilling, however, to sell high-quality cars because they believe these are likely to be undervalued. Buyers, based on the sellers' inferred unwillingness to sell high-quality cars, conclude that the cars they find in the market are low in quality and are unwilling to pay a high price even for a high-quality car. Fearing that they might pay an excessively high price for a lemon, they are unwilling to participate in the market.

Moral hazard occurs when a less-informed party to a transaction is unable to observe actions taken by another, more-informed party, which shifts the transaction's value away from the former.[2] Kenneth Arrow, in an example involving insurance, shows that people who are insured tend to take less care of themselves because they do not bear the costs of careless behavior. They shift these costs to other parties such as their insurance companies and other premium-paying policyholders.

We can find the same problems in financial markets, where adverse selection arises before a financial transaction (*ex ante*), and moral hazard afterward (*ex post*). The valuation of financial instruments such as stocks and bonds is inherently uncertain in that one must assess information held asymmetrically by firms and investors based on intangible, contractual rights rooted in corporate law. If this asymmetry is left as it is, the same problems will occur in the financial markets as well.

In a situation of adverse selection, only low-quality firms, or lemons, that deserve a low valuation are willing to participate in the financial markets as issuers of stocks and bonds. High-quality firms stay away, fearing an undeserved undervaluation. Investors, meanwhile, come to believe that only low-quality firms are to be found in the financial markets, and are unwilling to pay high prices even for truly high-quality firms as they have no means of verifying their quality. The reluctance of investors to pay keeps high-quality firms away from the market and deprives them of an avenue for raising capital.

---

[1]Akerlof, G. A. (1970). The market for "lemons": Quality uncertainty and the market mechanism. *Quarterly Journal of Economics*, 84(3), 488–500.

[2]Arrow, K. (1963). Uncertainty and the welfare economics of medical care. *American Economic Review*, 53(5), 941–973.

Moral hazard comes into play when firms have the means to harm their investors post-transaction and investors are aware of that possibility. Investors are reluctant to invest, and firms suffer from a lack of the capital necessary to undertake value-creating projects. This situation harms investors as well by reducing their opportunities for high-quality investment.

It is undesirable for both sides to leave the problem unsolved. When the functioning of financial markets is impaired under asymmetric information, firms fail to raise capital for desirable projects and investors fail to find desirable investments. Here we see both sides desiring to mitigate asymmetric information for their own benefit. While it is impossible to perfectly resolve asymmetry as long as there are corporate boundaries and disparities between internal and external information, it is possible to mitigate it. There are direct and indirect avenues for this purpose, as we shall see in the following.

2. Mitigating Asymmetric Information

2.1. Disclosure rules

The most common avenue for mitigating asymmetry is mandatory **disclosure** rules designed by regulators. Listed firms are generally required to file quarterly financial performance reports and additional material information in between, and investors are aware of this. This requirement ensures that key information is revealed to the public, and to that extent it mitigates asymmetry between firms and investors. Further, the rule of fair disclosure, which requires firms to disclose information in a timely manner when sharing it with any investor, assures investors of equal treatment in regard to information. Thanks to these measures, investors remain willing to participate in the markets and firms expect they will be given a fair evaluation to the extent that asymmetry is resolved. The role of disclosure regulations and their credible enforcement thus lies in mitigating asymmetric information. In this situation, high-quality firms can be less concerned about receiving an undeservedly low evaluation, and participate more willingly in the markets. Disclosure rules work after a transaction as well, by allowing investors to monitor firms using mitigated asymmetric information.

In addition to disclosure rules, there are regulations on **insider trading**, which ban insiders from trading securities based on material information unavailable to the public. Governments differ in their ideas on what constitutes insider information. When we broadly define the scope of insiders and insider information, we limit access to a universe of investors and keep private information from being reflected in the price of securities. With a narrow definition, we allow participants with private information to profit unfairly from securities trading, and general investors, concerned that their relative lack of information might place them in an inferior position, are inhibited from participating in the markets.

Legal scholars are not in consensus about the desirable degree of restriction on insider trading. Evidence is inconclusive on the effects of insider trading regulations, as measured by the bid–ask spreads of securities in the market which reflect degrees of market participation and transaction costs.[3] There are also differences in the degree to which insider trading regulations are enforced. The United States, for example, has more enforcement actions than other advanced economies.[4] This is partly because of differences in statutory preference: In Europe and Japan, where the burden of proof is comparatively strict, criminal sanctions by prosecutors are preferred over civil sanctions, such as the many class actions seen in the U.S.

This also relates to the **fair disclosure** rule. If analysts and institutional investors can obtain private, undisclosed corporate information, they may be able to profit from trading in the securities of firms relying on the undisclosed information, or publish reports based on it to benefit their client investors. Firms may also try to use this information gap as a bargaining tool, obtaining favorable evaluations or investments from analysts or investors in return for helpful tips. A fair disclosure rule prohibits these attempts as it requires firms to make information already conveyed to an outsider available to the public in a timely manner. This not only ensures fairness, but inspires confidence in the general investment community that the playing field is level, at least in terms of information. For the general investor, this translates into a continued willingness to take part in the markets.

---

[3] Bhattacharya, U. (2014). Insider trading controversies: A literature review. *Annual Review of Financial Economics*, 6, 385–403.
[4] Enriques, L., Hertig, G., Kanda, H., and Pargendler, M. (2017). Related party transactions. In R. Kraakman, J. Armour, P. Davies, L. Enriques, H. Hansmann, G. Hertig, H. Kanda, M. Pargendler, W. G. Ringe, and E. Rock (eds.), *The Anatomy of Corporate Law: A Comparative and Functional Approach*, 3rd ed. Oxford, UK: Oxford University Press, pp. 145–169.

2.2. Signaling

A second means of mitigating asymmetric information is **signaling**. When a firm wants to pass information to investors, it must assure them of the credibility of that information. A firm might try to please investors by issuing forecasts that are optimistic but lacking in any solid grounds. It is hard, however, for investors to verify the truth of information that firms convey. For instance, even when a firm wants to assure investors that its outlook is favorable, limits on information and uncertainty over the future mean that investors have only limited avenues by which to verify the firm's claims. One means of dealing with this is through signaling. Information conveyed directly by words may be hard to verify, but a firm can convey information indirectly by its own actions.

One common action is to pay **dividends**. As long as a firm commits to paying a stable stream of dividends, it sends a signal to investors that its performance outlook and cash flow sources are stable as well. This action is based on a general understanding in the financial markets that once a firm starts to pay dividends, any reduction in them will be negatively perceived in the markets,[5] while any increase will be perceived positively. Firms are careful, therefore, not to let dividends deteriorate. The effect is larger for a complete initiation and omission of dividends than for partial changes.[6] If a firm cuts its dividends, this sends a signal that it is growing less optimistic about its future cash flow, and investors may lower their internal valuation of the firm by reading the signal as a less-than-sanguine outlook.

Indeed, 80 percent of firms consider the signaling effect of dividends when setting payout policy.[7] This is why firms are reluctant to cut dividends even when they do have a less than optimistic outlook or face financial constraints. Given these effects, a firm's commitment to paying dividends reveals its confidence that it can generate enough cash flow to continue to pay them. This is a credible signal for investors to read. Here, it is worth noting that corporate information is ultimately revealed. The

[5]Grullon, G., Michaely, R., and Swaminathan, B. (2002). Are dividend changes a sign of firm maturity? *Journal of Business*, 75(3), 387–424.

[6]Michaely, R., Thaler, R. H., and Womack, K. L. (1995). Price reactions to dividend initiations and omissions: Overreaction or drift? *Journal of Finance*, 50(2), 573–608.

[7]Brav, A., Graham, J. R., Harvey, C. R., and Michaely, R. (2005). Payout policy in the 21st century. *Journal of Financial Economics*, 77(3), 483–527.

information conveyed by dividends, for instance, is revealed through the disclosure of a firm's financial performance, including the actual cash flow generated for investors.

Similarly, a **share repurchase** signals that a firm believes its shares to be undervalued. Given that firms have more information than investors, they are likely to repurchase shares only when they find them traded at below what they believe to be their true value. In contrast, firms hold off repurchasing shares when they believe them to be overvalued. Unlike the situation with dividend payments, firms have more discretion over whether and when they conduct repurchases. Given this flexibility, a firm's decision to repurchase shares sends a signal to investors that it believes its shares to be undervalued. Indeed, the financial markets react positively to announcements of share repurchase programs.[8]

2.3. Financial intermediaries

A third avenue is the use of **financial intermediaries**. There are a variety of such firms, professionals who process corporate information that has been disclosed either publicly or privately. An example of a processor of public information is the financial analyst. Financial analysts examine information that firms have made public, process the disclosed materials, and rate the firms on that basis. They often conduct interviews as well.

In contrast, financial intermediaries such as investment banks and credit rating agencies process private information. Investment banks process information when they underwrite equities, bonds, and other corporate securities based on information disclosed to them privately. They then market these securities to their client investors along with their analysis and evaluation. Their credibility is reinforced by their underwriting the securities, an act which shows commitment to taking a position based on the information they obtain. Similarly, credit rating agencies evaluate the creditworthiness of corporate debt securities, basing their assessment on private information disclosed to them alone under a confidentiality agreement. These financial intermediaries play roles in processing public and private information for the sake of investors who rely on their analysis and evaluation for investment decisions.

---

[8]Grullon, G. and Michaely, R. (2002). Dividends, share repurchases, and the substitution hypothesis. *Journal of Finance*, 57(4), 1649–1684.

Other types of financial intermediaries collect capital from investors and allocate them to firms, processing information in the course of doing so. Commercial banks act as financial intermediaries in that they allocate money taken as deposits through lending and investments based on their analysis and evaluation of firms. In essence, this means that they process corporate information on behalf of their depositors. Investment firms also play this type of role, as they set up mutual funds and other vehicles to invest money they collect from underlying investors based on the results of their information processing.

As a whole, these entities play an intermediary role between firms and investors in terms of information. Investors rely on the analyses and evaluations they produce in the form of analyst reports and credit ratings, as well as their underwriting and marketing activities. All of this serves to mitigate asymmetric information to the extent that investors find the information produced by these financial intermediaries to be credible. Firms also benefit from their performing these roles, as evaluations enable them to make transactions with investors on the basis of mitigated asymmetric information. It is noteworthy that firms pay underwriters and credit rating agencies, for instance, to process their private information. They do so because the benefits exceed the costs. Firms expend significant funds on dealing with these intermediaries and disclosing private information. And, through their borrowing costs and financing fees, the firms that raise funds through these intermediaries essentially bear the costs of mitigating asymmetric information. Underlying investors share the costs by accepting interest rates on deposits that are lower than those charged for borrowers and by paying management fees and commissions to invest in mutual funds. Collectively, both firms and investors pay these intermediaries to mitigate asymmetric information.

The role played by financial intermediaries is based on the belief that **confidentiality** is warranted. Professional firms that share and process private corporate information are usually bound by confidentiality agreements. The belief that a contract will be honored by its parties thus underlies such intermediation. Further, the credibility of a financial intermediary hinges on its **reputation**. Given the intangible nature of financial advice and decisions, building and protecting one's reputation is key to the survival of a financial intermediary. If investors see that a financial intermediary is causing them losses by producing low-quality information or prioritizing its own interest over theirs, the intermediary's reputation will be damaged along with its competitiveness in the markets.

Investors can rely on information produced by financial intermediaries because of the latter's incentive to maintain a good reputation in a competitive marketplace.

Part of this mechanism is reinforced by laws in the form of **fiduciary duties** imposed on financial intermediaries offering services to firms and investors. Their relationship to the structure of corporate governance is discussed in Chapter 7.

2.4. Financial instruments

A fourth avenue is found in the choice and design of **financial instruments**. Financial instruments like **debt** and **equity**, and their hybrid forms such as convertible bonds and preferred shares, incorporate different conditions and consequences into their design. These differences provide firms with different incentives. For instance, debt, unlike equity, has a predetermined schedule of repayment. Owing to this property, the choice of debt carries a credible signal about stable future cash flow.[9] If a firm attempts to renege on its promise after a debt transaction — a typical moral hazard case — it faces the risk of bankruptcy or reorganization should its debtholders take over its assets. This is ensured by reliable **bankruptcy codes**, which give firms a credible disincentive to renege. Therefore, when a firm expects a predictable stream of cash flow in the future, it can convey this information to investors by choosing to issue debt, rather than equity.

To put it another way, investors infer information from signals that firms convey by their choice of financial instruments. By choosing debt, they signal that they anticipate a stable cash flow, in terms of timing and amount, that is sufficient to repay their debts in the future. Firms with a less optimistic outlook would rather avoid issuing debt. Instead, they choose equity, which does not require them to commit to the timing of future cash flow payments and thus does not entail the threat of bankruptcy.

Debt instruments have a variety of design options. A debt instrument can be either secured or unsecured. When a firm issues a **secured** debt instrument, it is putting its assets at stake in a structured manner for the

---

[9]Ross, S. (1977). The determination of financial structure: The incentive-signalling approach. *Bell Journal of Economics*, 8(1), 23–40.

benefit of specific investors. This conveys to them a credible signal that the firm is willing to keep its promise, because otherwise it will lose its assets. Such signals are important, especially for firms with low credit ratings and a higher probability of default. Also, debt can carry **covenants** that restrict firms' actions or subject them to debtholders' approval, such as limits on mergers, change of control, sales of assets, and the amounts of capital expenditure and additional debt issued. Covenants may also oblige firms to keep certain metrics under control, such as their debt-to-equity ratio, annual earnings, and credit rating of debt.[10] Further, if a firm chooses **short-term** rather than long-term debt, investors are able to see changes in the firm's circumstances reflected in subsequent renewal transactions. Therefore, a firm's choice of short-term debt sends a signal that it is unlikely to harm investors, while investors will not require the compensation for potential moral hazards that would be required for long-term debt.[11]

In some cases, debt may also incorporate a **call option**, under which a firm may redeem debt at its own discretion. In return for obtaining such an option, the firm repays its investors in the form of a higher interest rate on debt than would apply without such an option. This conveys another signal that the firm expects its creditworthiness to improve before its debt reaches maturity — otherwise, the firm would have no reason to pay for such an option. This is especially true when interest rates are set as the sum of a floating market rate and a spread based on a firm's creditworthiness, in which case a call option is valuable only when a firm believes that the spread will fall after a transaction, reflecting an improvement in its creditworthiness.

When the size of a pie is fixed, a behavior that harms debt investors often benefits shareholders, and vice versa, thus affecting the slicing of the pie. If investors are uncertain as to which position will serve them best, they may prefer to invest in **hybrid securities**, such as convertible bonds or preferred shares, and thus enjoy the best of both worlds. These hybrids offer the properties of debt and equity in one instrument. Their hybrid features give investors the comfort of knowing that their positions

---

[10]Chava, S., Kumar, P., and Warga, A. (2010). Managerial agency and bond covenants. *Review of Financial Studies*, 23(3), 1120–1148.
[11]Myers, S. C. (1977). Determinants of corporate borrowing. *Journal of Financial Economics*, 5(2), 147–175.

will not be harmed as long as either can be used to their benefit through whichever actions a firm chooses to take.

In the case of **convertible bonds**, investors have the right to convert their holdings into common shares. If a firm takes an action which benefits shareholders at the expense of debtholders, investors in convertible bonds can exercise their right to switch position to the shareholder side and thus share in their benefit. Given this protection, for a firm to issue convertible bonds sends a signal to investors that it does not intend to harm its debtholders.[12]

While **preferred shares** have a variety of design options as well, these typically have a redemption clause that allows investors to recoup their investment, often at a multiple of the original amount, before any payment is made to investors in common shares. This is accompanied by the right to convert their holdings into common shares by a predetermined ratio. The conversion ratio often provides protection from **dilution** through future rounds of additional issues of common or preferred shares. These dual properties give investors an avenue to recover their investment in a similar manner to debt, while having an upside similar to that offered by equity.

Overall, the choice of one of these financial instruments sends the signal that a firm does not intend to harm its investors after a transaction. Moral hazards are thus avoided and comfort given to investors working under conditions of asymmetric information. In the sense that its contractual arrangements matter more than its verbal statements, the firm's actions speak louder than words.

3. Asymmetric Information in Initial Public Offerings

3.1. Initial public offering underpricing

One occasion where asymmetric information is considerable is the **initial public offering (IPO)**. Unlike the situation with a secondary equity offering, where a listed firm issues additional shares, investors in an IPO do not have existing market information to rely on when evaluating these new entrants to the public markets.

---

[12]Chakraborty, A. and Yilmaz, B. (2011). Adverse selection and convertible bonds. *Review of Economic Studies*, 78(1), 148–175.

Typically, investment banks are assigned as **underwriters**, whose job is to guarantee that firms sell all of the shares offered by undertaking to purchase all of them before selling them down to investors even if part of them are left unsold. By means of a marketing and book-building process, underwriters then ask their clients, which include sophisticated institutional investors, about their potential demand for the shares. The underwriters estimate a range of share prices offered to match supply with demand, and, based on their advice, firms decide on a final price at which to offer their shares. Underwriters decide which investors will be allocated shares based on orders they have received up to that time. If demand exceeds supply, some of the orders may be filled at the underwriters' discretion, or they may exercise a *greenshoe* option, which is a call option granted to them beforehand to sell additional shares issued by the firm.

After the listing, investment banks provide market support for the stock price in the aftermarket and initiate coverage by analysts who report on firms regularly to maintain the interest of investors and thereby the liquidity of the stock.

Underpricing occurring at the time of an IPO is a phenomenon where newly traded shares experience a first-day pop-up in price on the stock exchange against the decided offered price. When this happens, it means that a listed firm has left money on the table, because there would be no pop-up if the shares were fairly priced. In the U.S. equity market alone, underpricing averaging 18.9 percent existed from 1980 to 2021, leaving a total of $229.7 billion on the table.[13] Similar phenomena have been observed consistently in other 53 countries, ranging from Argentina to Switzerland.[14] This also means that the investors to which underwriters have allocated shares enjoy an instant gain on the first day of trading. Asymmetric information can give rise to mispricing, in which some shares are undervalued but others overvalued. On average, however, this should produce no meaningful difference from zero in their first-day returns. Therefore, the observed facts suggest that IPOs are consistently underpriced.

There are a number of explanations as to why this might happen, though they are not mutually exclusive. A plausible one is that underwriters

---

[13] Ritter, J. R. (2022). Initial public offerings: Updated statistics, *IPO Data*, February 1, 2022.
[14] Loughran, T., Ritter, J. R., and Rydqvist, K. (1994). Initial public offerings: International insights. *Pacific-Basin Finance Journal*, 2(2–3), 165–199, and their update, March 3, 2022.

favor client investors at the expense of client firms. Selling a valuable investment at a discount certainly benefits one's client investors, and underwriters can expect benefits, such as future orders, in return from improved relationships.

Alternatively, given the initial uncertainties in pricing, underwriters may need sophisticated investors to give them accurate information to use in evaluating firms, as a mistake in pricing can mean losses in the form of an inventory of unsold shares. If investors know they will have to pay a price they have committed to with their underwriters, they will be reluctant to state the true price. Rather, they will have an incentive to state a lower price than they believe to be accurate. Underpricing may be the price paid by underwriters to investors for valuable information. If investors believe they will be fairly compensated for revealing accurate information in the form of underpricing, they are incentivized to share that information with underwriters. And since underwriters need accurate information, they are willing to offer compensation, even at the expense of their client firms.

Even investors face significant uncertainty in evaluating and investing in firms. Although a book-building process is not an auction, it has similar characteristics in that investors willing to pay more are likely to have more shares allocated to them, and vice versa. In this process, investors may come to fear that they are overpaying. This is the situation called **winner's curse**. The phenomenon originates from an observation of auctions for the right to drill oil wells in the U.S.,[15] where winning bidders actually suffered losses afterward.

In an IPO, investors bidding higher prices ultimately receive allocations of shares in a process similar to an auction. Here, too, investors may suffer a loss despite apparent success in bidding if the winning price exceeds the true price. In contrast, low-bidding investors who failed to receive shares may actually turn out to be better off in that they have avoided overpaying. Fearing susceptibility to winner's curse, investors tend to underprice, rather than overprice, the shares in which they are interested, causing systematically observed underpricing.

Further, when sophisticated investors refrain from bidding high, unsophisticated investors, rather than outbid them, tend to follow suit, believing that experienced investors are better informed and can more precisely

---

[15]Capen, E. C., Clapp, R. V., and Campbell, W. M. (1971). Competitive bidding in high-risk situations. *Journal of Petroleum Technology*, 23(6), 641–653.

evaluate shares. Otherwise, only unsophisticated investors would be allocated shares, leading to winner's curse. This herding behavior results in an **information cascade**, with all participants taking the same course of action and amplifying the systematic underpricing observed in IPOs.

3.2. Alternative listing avenues

Insofar as underpricing occurs, firms will be worse off, because it is new shareholders who take the money left on the table in first-day pop-ups — even if the firm's founders and early investors enjoy long-awaited capital gains from their investments and the liquidity of their holdings. Systematic underpricing makes firms less willing to go public, and some avenues have evolved to deal with this phenomenon.

3.2.1. Auction

Given that underpricing occurs at a point between the pricing by an under-writer and that by investors trading on the stock exchange, one straight-forward solution is to conduct **auctions** for prospective investors. This is what Google (now Alphabet) tried in its IPO on the Nasdaq in 2004. Google did not go through the traditional process of book building by an underwriter. Instead, it conducted a Dutch auction, in which all bidders pricing their shares at or above the minimum price that matched the shares' demand and supply would pay the same minimum price. In Google's case, the price was set at $85, valuing the firm at $23 billion and allowing it to raise $1.67 billion at the same time. Moving the clock forward, we know that Alphabet's market capitalization exceeded $1 trillion for the first time in January 2020.[16]

The firm's listing attracted a lot of attention from investment communities, not only because it involved a high-profile Silicon Valley startup, but also because of its auction format. Investment banks were looking closely at the listing, because if many startups followed suit in bypassing underwriters, the mainstay of their business would suffer. Few firms did follow suit, however, sticking instead to the traditional process

---

[16]Ramkumar, A. (2020). Alphabet becomes fourth U.S. company to reach $1 trillion market value. *Bloomberg*, January 16, 2020.

of book building led by investment banks in their traditional role of underwriters.

3.2.2. Direct listing

Another avenue is the **direct listing**, a prominent example of which is the listing by Spotify, the music streaming service provider, in 2018. Spotify listed its shares directly on the New York Stock Exchange (NYSE) with a $29.5 billion valuation but without raising any capital. Other firms following Spotify included Slack, an office software provider based in Silicon Valley, and Palantir, a big data processing solution provider, which went public through direct listings on the NYSE in 2019 and 2020. Coinbase, a cryptocurrency exchange, followed suit in 2021 on the Nasdaq.

In a direct listing there are no lock-ups, a restriction typically accompanying the traditional IPO which prohibits existing shareholders from selling their holdings for the next 180 days. Without this restriction, direct listings provide existing shareholders with instant liquidity. No limits are placed on buyers, either, in that all prospective buyers have initial access to share trading, unlike in the traditional IPO which gives such access only to the client investors of the underwriter. Direct listing also does not require road shows, a costly process that firms go on the road with their underwriters to meet with key institutional investors in large cities, sometimes globally, to promote potential sales of their shares.

A direct listing has some advantages over traditional underwriting. First and most obviously, it avoids underpricing by leaving the price formation process to the stock exchange at the time of listing. By definition, there is no first-day pop-up because there is no price predetermined by sellers and buyers. Unlike a traditional IPO, wherein underwriters have a strong say in deciding the offered price by standing between firms and their client investors, a direct listing matches supply and demand — literally directly — at the stock exchange, with the help of market makers at the time of an opening auction on the exchange. Shares start trading when the bid and ask prices submitted by prospective buyers and sellers match.

Second, direct listings save firms fees that would otherwise be paid to investment banks for their underwriting services, typically set at 7 percent of equity value regardless of the absolute amount. This fixed ratio remains a puzzle, since in a competitive market fees for large issuers might be at a lower percentage, reflecting economies of scale in the analysis and evaluation of those firms, the preparation of required documents and materials, and communication with regulators and stock exchanges as well as marketing to investors. There is, however, no evidence of potential fee collusion among investment banks.[17]

In a direct listing, an investment bank will still play a role as an advisor to a firm, but often with a flat fee. It will still act as a financial intermediary in the sense of processing corporate information for the sake of investors, but the degree of its commitment and incentive is lower than in the traditional role of underwriter. As discussed, disclosure is a basic means of mitigating asymmetric information between firms and investors. Firms are required to provide the same level of disclosure as for a traditional IPO — an S-1 registration statement under the U.S. SEC rule, for example. In terms of information, it is primarily firms which fill in the gaps with investors. They do this by disclosing information, often by holding direct meetings with investors, with the help of their advisor investment banks.

In a direct listing, the diminished role of investment banks also means there is a weaker signaling effect. In a traditional IPO, underwriting serves as a signal that the underwriter is validating a firm through its financial commitment. In a direct listing, there is no intermediary to give a stamp of approval, no one validating the offer by risking a financial stake in the firm. The use of intermediaries thus rests on a balance: on the one hand, there are the benefits of quality assurance for uncertain investments; on the other, the direct costs of fees and the indirect costs of underpricing. This shows once more that there are costs entailed in mitigating asymmetric information. A direct listing reverses the benefits and costs, offering the new benefits of a simple, low-cost listing without fear of underpricing, but entailing the new costs of an absence of financial intermediaries to mitigate asymmetric information.

Direct listings were further deregulated in 2020. Prior to that, it had been understood that direct listings were for firms that needed no additional capital, but only liquidity; in that year, however, the SEC, responding to a request from the NYSE, allowed firms to raise capital through direct listings,[18] followed by similar changes by the Nasdaq the next

---

[17]Hansen, R. (2001). Do investment banks compete in IPOs? The advent of the '7% plus contract.' *Journal of Financial Economics*, 59(3), 313–346.
[18]The U.S. Securities and Exchange Commission (2020). Self-regulatory organizations; New York Stock Exchange LLC; Order approving a proposed rule change, as modified by

year.[19] Under the new rule, firms going public, as well as existing share-holders, can sell new shares directly on the stock exchange. Firms are permitted to set a price range in their registration statement, with the opening price limited to the lowest end of the range; otherwise, the primary direct listing may not proceed. In allowing firms to raise capital at the time of listing, the primary direct listing is closer to the traditional IPO, which typically involves issuing new shares to raise capital. However, as the lack of financial intermediaries can lead to insufficient investor protection in terms of information, additional regulations may follow in this regard.

3.2.3. *Special purpose acquisition companies*

Another alternative is to use a **special purpose acquisition company (SPAC)**. In 2019, Virgin Galactic, the space tourism venture founded by Sir Richard Branson in 2004, went public by merging with a blank-check company listed on the NYSE.[20] In 2021, Grab, a ride-hailing company, went public with a $40 billion valuation by merging with a SPAC listed on the Nasdaq.[21] SPACs are shell companies with liquid assets. They are listed with a limited lifetime, typically two years, with the sole purpose of merging and acquiring other firms with shareholder approval during this period; otherwise, they are liquidated. These shell companies are themselves listed through the traditional avenue of an IPO. SPACs raise capital from investors who do not know which business they will be investing in, and hold these funds in the form of liquid assets to pay for possible future deals sought by their managers or for redemptions at the investors'

---

amendment No. 2, to amend Chapter One of the Listed Company Manual to modify the provisions relating to direct listings. Release No. 34-89684; File No. SR-NYSE-2019-67.
[19]The U.S. Securities and Exchange Commission (2021). Self-regulatory organizations; The Nasdaq Stock Market LLC; Order approving a proposed rule change, as modified by amendment No. 2, to allow companies to list in connection with a direct listing with a primary offering in which the company will sell shares itself in the opening auction on the first day of trading on Nasdaq and to explain how the opening transaction for such a listing will be effected. Release No. 34-91947; File No. SR-NASDAQ-2020-057.
[20]Jasper, C. (2019). Branson's Virgin Galactic space venture jumps in NYSE debut. *Bloomberg*, October 28, 2019.
[21]Wang, Y. and Sebastian, D. (2021). Grab shares tumble in trading debut after blockbuster SPAC deal. *Wall Street Journal*, December 2, 2021.

request. Fundraising by SPACs surged in 2020, totaling $83.4 billion, more than six times greater than the $13.6 billion total of the year before.[22] However, the situation reversed in the middle of 2021, a year that recorded $161.8 billion, following the SEC's announcement of its intention to tighten regulation of the vehicles.[23]

The use of a SPAC means that firms going public do not go through the traditional process of preparing for an IPO because they simply merge with, or are acquired by, a SPAC. It is also less complicated for new, combined firms to raise capital while conducting a merger or acquisition, because SPACs, as listed firms, are only subject to regulations on additional share issues by listed firms.

By using a SPAC, a firm going public saves on costs that would otherwise be paid to financial intermediaries, such as underwriters, involved in the traditional process of an IPO. The firm benefits from knowing who its investors are when it goes public and is able to negotiate and agree beforehand on the price at which it will sell its shares, as in the deal negotiation process for a merger or acquisition. It need not be concerned about a potential underpricing beyond its control because it negotiates the price with the SPAC manager itself, possibly with help of a financial advisor. In other words, it has direct control over the process and no pricing uncertainty at the time of listing.

At the same time, given the blank-check nature of a SPAC, investor protection can be insufficient in that the investor has no advance knowledge of the firms it will be investing in, and, at the time of the resolution of the merger between the SPAC and the firm, lacks the level of information that would be disclosed if the firm were to go public through an IPO. It must rely on the manager of the SPAC for selection, valuation, and negotiation in regard to target firms. In this sense, the managers of SPACs are financial intermediaries who process information by standing between firms and investors. SPACs are thus similar to investment funds in their intermediary role, in that underlying investors evaluate the managers of the funds which process corporate information on their behalf. The reputation of managers is a key factor from this perspective.

---

[22] Statista Research Department (2022). Proceeds of special purpose acquisition company (SPAC) IPOs in the United States from 2003 to January 2022, February 2, 2022.
[23] The U.S. Securities and Exchange Commission (2021). SEC charges SPAC, sponsor, merger target, and CEOs for misleading disclosure ahead of proposed business combination, 2021-124.

Where asymmetric information is concerned, SPACs shift the burden from firms to investors, in the sense that firms need be less concerned about asymmetric information when negotiating with a SPAC. In a traditional IPO, prices are set by an underwriter who must meet the demands of a multitude of investors, potentially resulting in a low offer price that shields the underwriter from the risk of unsold share inventories, particularly at times of uncertain investor demand. This uncertainty in investor demand is also present in direct listings, where firms leave the valuation of their shares to the stock exchange at the time of listing. SPACs shift this uncertainty to the side of investors by raising capital beforehand and reaching agreement with firms afterward.

As a result, investors are concerned about the selection and prices of future target firms, precisely because these are things they cannot fully control. For this reason, there are litigations based on insufficient disclosure at the time of shareholder approval for a merger. Furthermore, SPACs structures typically cause dilution for investors by entitling managers to an additional stake of typically 20 percent without contributing capital, issuing warrants to original investors at no additional cost, and funding through private placements with new public investors during the search period in response to redemption by original investors.[24] These arrangements can undermine investor protections. However, investors are entitled to redemption with the full price of the units and interest rate, and the incentives of managers of SPACs are aligned with those of investors to the extent that they share a financial stake in their organization and they have an incentive to maintain their reputation.

This characteristic of pooled capital shares a major source of strength with investment funds, such as hedge funds. Regulations on SPACs, however, as operating companies seeking business combinations subject to shareholders' approval, are less stringent than those on investment funds, which have broader discretion in their investments and trades in securities.[25] What they have in common is that while managers have discretion over investment decisions, including selection and pricing, investors in these funds face a high degree of uncertainty, as they have no knowledge of what they will be investing in when they commit to them. They therefore assess the fund managers' strategies, skills, track records, and other credentials before making a commitment. In 2020, Bill Ackman, manager

[24]Klausner, M., Ohlrogge, M., and Ruan, E. (2022). A sober look at SPACs. *Yale Journal on Regulation*, 39(1), 228–303.
[25]Sections 3(a)(1)(A) and (C), The Investment Company Act of 1940.

of the hedge fund Pershing Square, founded a SPAC for which he raised $4 billion — a record at the time,[26] although it resulted in the failure of a target deal with Universal Music; and lawsuits over the vehicle's course of action.[27]

Given that SPACs shift the burden to investors, stock exchange regulations on the listing of SPACs and disclosure requirements at the time of merger are important issues for investor protection. A stringent disclosure requirement at the time of merger would allow investors to evaluate the selection and the pricing of the target firm, rather than rely only on the reputation of investment managers. Such a requirement would bring SPAC deals closer to the IPOs, in that investors would be informed of what they are committing themselves to. There would not, however, be an equivalent intermediary role by underwriters to test the validity of the information, as this role would be played by managers. This itself is a consequence of shifting the burden of redressing asymmetric information.

What we observe is a diversifying range of avenues for firms to go public, with the traditional process of the IPO not standing on its own. While traditional IPOs remain the mainstream, these multiple avenues are unlikely to merge into any single method. Instead, they will coexist in the financial markets, supported by advancements in technology and greater ease in obtaining and processing information than in the days when investment bankers dominated the arena with phone calls and visits to firms and institutional investors. The traditional role of financial intermediaries is being replaced by alternative avenues of direct communication. These are between firms and potential investors in the case of direct listings, and between firms and managers of already listed entities in the case of SPACs.

4. Asymmetric Information and the Agency Problem

4.1. *Agency problem*

Asymmetric information exists not only at the level of financial markets as a whole. It is also present at the firm level between managers and

---

[26]Nivedita, C. and Franklin, J. (2020). Ackman-backed blank check company's units rise in NYSE debut. *Reuters*, July 22, 2020.

[27]Sorkin, A. R. *et al.* (2021). Bill Ackman's SPAC gets sued. *New York Times*, August 17, 2021.

shareholders, particularly as a moral hazard occurring after a transaction. This type of moral hazard is called the **agency problem**, where actions by managers as agents deviate from the interests of shareholders as principals. The concept was formalized in the 1970s by Michael Jensen and William Meckling.[28]

The asymmetry of information between shareholders and managers is based on the **separation of ownership and control**, by which shareholders delegate corporate management to professional managers. Under this structure, managers can invest in businesses even when they lack capital, while shareholders can rely on the managerial skills of others when deploying their capital. Shareholders control the relationship through approvals at shareholders' meetings, where the board of directors, which includes top managers such as CEOs, are elected.

This separation, however, causes asymmetric information in that shareholders do not have full access to a firm's internal information while managers do. Shareholders in a listed firm rely on the firm's disclosure for information on that firm, and, unless managers and shareholders agree otherwise, disclosure may be limited to the extent that managers desire discretion vis-à-vis their shareholders. This limit on disclosure translates into additional costs for shareholders who wish to obtain and verify information or set contractual arrangements to align managers' incentives with theirs. This structure also involves the issue of **bargaining** between managers and shareholders, as managers may not want close monitoring or limits on their discretion, despite shareholders being entitled to various rights under corporate laws and articles of incorporation. To the extent that shareholders rely on managers' skills for the success of their investments, managers have bargaining power in the ability to keep some information private, as well as having discretion in making managerial decisions.

This information gap creates an incentive for managers to benefit not shareholders, but themselves. Managers may be driven by financial motives, as well as the social one of establishing status among their industry peers, to give themselves excessive pay and perks. Or, they may aspire to the management of large firms rather than small ones, incentivizing them to make less efficient investments in a move toward **empire building**. In making project decisions, they may select investment projects that

---

[28] Jensen, M. C. and Meckling, W. H. (1976). Theory of the firm: Managerial behavior, agency costs and ownership structure. *Journal of Financial Economics*, 3(4), 305–360.

call for more of their own skills, thus keeping them essential to the firm, and pass over value-maximizing projects that require the skills of others. Further, they may make it hard for their firms to be acquired, even when the acquisition would benefit shareholders, because a change of control might threaten their position. On top of these forms of self-protection, they may seek a "quiet life" by avoiding desirable risk-taking that would be beneficial to shareholders.[29] These are examples of **management entrenchment**, a behavior by managers seeking to keep their positions at the expense of shareholders.

Shareholders cannot always have their own way. Monitoring and verifying the actions of managers involves bargaining, is costly, and can be against their interests. If managers and shareholders could write a contract that perfectly compensated the managers' efforts, managers would have no incentive to deviate from it. However, given the complexity and uncertainty of the managerial environment, it is impossible to write a precise contract that takes into consideration all possible future events and thus prevents such a deviation.

Some remedies exist to deal with this problem. As is the case with avenues to mitigate asymmetric information to avoid adverse selection and moral hazard in the financial markets, remedies to mitigate asymmetry between managers and shareholders are beneficial for both sides. If investors believe that managers will harm them after a transaction occurs, they will be unwilling to invest their capital in firms, and managers and entrepreneurs will lack the capital to run and start businesses. Investors will also lose opportunities to profit from investments in the talent and ideas of other people.

A typical solution is performance-linked pay, which ties compensation to the performance of stock prices. For instance, restricted stock and stock options, which vest in, say, five years, align the incentives of managers with those of shareholders to lift the value of shares. However, pay-performance sensitivity is typically not high, as measured by a pay change of $3.25 for every $1,000 change in shareholders' wealth.[30]

Shareholders are also able to press for the replacement of poorly performing CEOs. CEO turnover is related to stock performance, whether

---

[29]Bertrand, M. and Mullainathan, S. (2003). Enjoying the quiet life? Corporate governance and managerial preferences. *Journal of Political Economy*, 111(5), 1043–1075.
[30]Jensen, M. C. and Murphy, K. J. (1990). Performance pay and top-management incentives. *Journal of Political Economy*, 98(2), 225–264.

forced or unforced.[31] This pressure causes managers to act for the benefit of shareholders. Boards of directors, in particular those dominated by outsiders, are more likely to replace a CEO after witnessing bad performance.[32] This is not one-sided, however, because CEOs also have bargaining power as members of boards of directors, and replacing them is costly.[33] This allows CEOs to seek entrenchment to some extent.[34]

One of the main purposes of corporate governance design, which we shall discuss in Chapter 7, is to mitigate problems that arise from asymmetric information held by managers and shareholders. The construct of corporate governance takes into consideration a balance struck between managers and shareholders. On the one hand, if the architecture of corporate governance allows for manager entrenchment, it erodes investor confidence in firms and makes them less willing to participate in the financial markets. Stronger corporate governance rules give better protection to investors and motivate them to continue investing in the financial markets. On the other hand, if regulation is too stringent in favor of investors, managers will be unwilling to run public firms, and will choose instead to remain or go private. Managers and entrepreneurs may even be discouraged from starting businesses, as it will be too costly and risky for them to do so. Again, this balance reflects the fact that to mitigate asymmetric information in the financial markets and among firms is an expensive proposition, one that involves managerial incentives and bargaining power. In this case, the degree of investor protection rests on a balance between the benefits and costs entailed in mitigating such an asymmetry.

5. Conclusion

Asymmetric information exists everywhere in the financial markets both before and after transactions, causing adverse selection in the first case and moral hazard in the second. Information gaps are ultimately filled in,

---

[31]Kaplan, S. N. and Minton, B. A. (2011). How has CEO turnover changed? *International Review of Finance*, 12(1), 57–87.

[32]Weisbach, M. S. (1988). Outside directors and CEO turnover. *Journal of Financial Economics*, 20(1–2), 431–460.

[33]Hermalin, B. E. and Weisbach, M. S. (1998). Endogenously chosen boards of directors and their monitoring of the CEO. *American Economic Review*, 88(1), 96–118.

[34]Taylor, L. A. (2010). Why are CEOs rarely fired? Evidence from structural estimation. *Journal of Finance*, 65(6), 2051–2087.

initially with private information revealed to investors over time. But it is in the interest of all parties to mitigate asymmetry in order to avoid such undesirable consequences as high-quality firms refraining from participating in the financial markets or desirable projects being passed over. Financial intermediaries play important roles in filling information gaps by processing information and facilitating transactions. Asymmetries are also mitigated by regulations, including disclosure rules, restrictions on insider trading, and bankruptcy codes, and by private contracts such as confidentiality agreements and debt covenants. They originate from the understanding that investors face real-world friction in terms of information.

Asymmetric information also exists between managers and shareholders, creating an agency problem under the separation of ownership and control. Bargaining between managers, who may seek discretion and entrenchment, and investors, who need protection against managers, results in corporate governance design that promotes better alignment and benefits both sides.

These measures and institutional arrangements are not static, however. As we have seen in novel use cases of direct listings and SPACs as alternatives to mitigate underpricing in IPOs, new measures and contractual arrangements continue to be devised and tried out in efforts to better resolve the problem of asymmetric information and facilitate the participation of firms and investors in the financial markets.

Chapter 4

Optimizing Capital Structure

1. Debt and Equity

Firms fund investment projects by issuing securities, such as debt and equity, or by borrowing from banks. **Capital structure** theory deals with how firms decide on the combination of financial instruments they will use and the impact of their choices. **Debt** is the oldest form of financing, appearing in the 5th century BC in the ancient Roman code The Law of Twelve Tables.[1] **Equity**, by contrast, came about with the concept of a corporation that originated with the Dutch East India Company in 1602.

A key property of equity is **limited liability**. At the beginning, limited liability was primarily meant to indemnify the king from the liabilities of state-run firms.[2] Distribution of profits according to ownership share is a unique property of equity which is unseen in debt. Even before corporations came into being, the concept of sharing the fruits of business in return for investment already existed. It was seen in partnerships, whose shares, however, came with unlimited liability for owners. Limited liability for corporations brought the format into the mainstream, enabling investors to limit their risk to the amount they contribute.

---

[1] Johnson, A. C., Coleman-Norton, P. R., Bourne, C., and Pharr, C. (eds.) (2003). *Ancient Roman Statutes: A Translation with Introduction, Commentary, Glossary, and Index.* Clark, NJ: Lawbook Exchange.

[2] Bainbridge, S. M. and Henderson, M. T. (2016). *Limited Liability: A Legal and Economic Analysis.* Cheltenham, UK: Edward Elgar.

One difference between debt and equity concerns seniority in the recovery of investments from corporate assets, where debt is prioritized over equity. This difference becomes important when a firm falls into financial distress, and debt holders can act to recover their investment by selling corporate assets, ultimately through court proceedings. Equity holders, in contrast, are subordinated to debt holders, but are entitled to receive all assets that remain after debt is paid off. This makes them **residual claimants** to assets. They also have the right to control a firm's decision through voting, such as for the election of directors and for corporate reorganization by mergers and other means.

Presented with the choice of financial instruments represented by debt and equity, each with its different characteristics, firms must decide on the best combination to use. The choice they make forms the **capital structure** of the firm. As this choice is made for the purpose of funding its capital investments, a firm's primary interest is the resulting cost of capital against the profitability of investments. Generally, debt is a cheaper financial instrument than equity because it has seniority over equity, and because its maturity and return are determined beforehand by means of contracts, giving it greater certainty and predictability. In reality, however, too much debt leads a firm into financial distress, so one needs to aim for an optimal mix of debt and equity. While this mix may be elusive, the theory established by Modigliani and Miller provides a helpful starting point.

2. The Modigliani–Miller Theorem

The proposition set forth by Franco Modigliani and Merton Miller was that capital structure is irrelevant to the cost of capital and therefore to the value of a firm. Hence it is called the **Modigliani–Miller (MM) irrelevance theorem**.[3] It posits that capital structure decisions affect neither the business risk of firms nor their cost of capital as a whole. As seen in Chapter 1, firm value is obtained as the present value of future free cash flow discounted by the cost of capital. If the cost of capital is not affected by capital structure, neither is firm value, as long as free cash flow is unchanged. This is intuitive in the sense that the intrinsic business of a

---

[3] Modigliani, F. and Miller, M. H. (1958). The cost of capital, corporation finance and the theory of investment. *American Economic Review*, 48(3), 261–297.

firm is irrelevant to the mix of debt and equity selected by its managers. For instance, the performance of a restaurant depends on the selection of such factors as the chef, menu, and location in a competitive local market, but presumably not on the mix of debt and equity used to finance the business. Similarly, the attractiveness of a gadget lies in its design and function, but not in how its purchase is financed. This irrelevance means that free cash flow from business operations is not affected by the manner in which such operations are financed, but only by intrinsic business decisions such as a change in chef, menu, or location. First proposed in the late 1950s, the irrelevance theorem became a fundamental mode of thought on the capital structure of firms, one that continues to be applied in business practices today.

The basic result of Modigliani–Miller's irrelevance theorem is that the cost of equity capital rises in accordance with leverage to compensate for increasing risk, and that it offsets the benefits of increasing debt. This is intuitive given that equity capital cushions changes in corporate earnings, and, when at a low level, raises the likelihood of insolvency. Reflecting the rise in equity cost, the total cost of capital remains constant, even if a firm takes on more debt as a cheaper source of capital. This is because the equity cost rises to the extent that its risk is affected, neutralizing the effect of cheaper capital. This neutrality should hold true as long as there is no change in the intrinsic riskiness of the firm's business, which is affected by operating decisions rather than financial decisions.

Let us see how the proportional change in the cost of equity to leverage occurs. Figure 4.1 shows the relationship between the costs of capital (vertical axis) and leverage, measured by the debt-to-equity ratio (horizontal axis), assuming a constant cost of capital required for firm assets (r_A). We also assume a constant cost of capital required for debt (r_D), meaning that the firm is able to borrow as much as it wants at the same rate, and no corporate tax for the firm. We shall relax this assumption of constant debt cost and no corporate tax later on.

When a firm has no leverage, meaning that it finances its assets wholly with equity, the cost of equity capital (r_E) is equal to the cost of its assets. We call this cost the **unlevered cost of capital**. It is the rate of return that investors require to take on the business risk of a firm's assets, such as the risk level of its free cash flow. When leverage rises, the share of cheaper debt capital increases, apparently lowering the whole cost of capital *per se*. However, the cost of equity capital also rises enough to compensate for the increasing risk, thereby neutralizing the total effect.

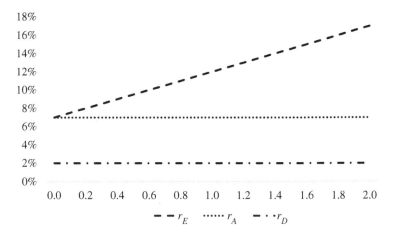

Figure 4.1   Leverage and cost of equity.

The algebraic relationship between the costs of capital and leverage is as follows:

$$r_E = r_A + (r_A - r_D)\frac{V_D}{V_E}$$

where r_E is the cost of equity, r_A is the unlevered cost of capital, r_D is the cost of debt, and V_D and V_E are the market value of debt and equity, respectively. The cost of equity in Figure 4.1 is computed by assuming that the unlevered cost of capital is 7 percent and the cost of debt is 2 percent. This relationship is equivalent to the expression that the unlevered cost of capital, which is constant, is the weighted average of the cost of debt and the cost of equity:

$$r_A = r_D\frac{V_D}{V_A} + r_E\frac{V_E}{V_A}$$

where V_A is the market value of firm assets. This equation also represents a formula for calculating the weighted average cost of capital (WACC) of a firm in a state with no tax.

Next, let us relax the assumption of the constant cost of debt by assuming instead that it rises with leverage. This is more realistic, because the likelihood of default on debt increases with higher leverage, for which debt investors require a higher rate of return. Figure 4.2 shows this result,

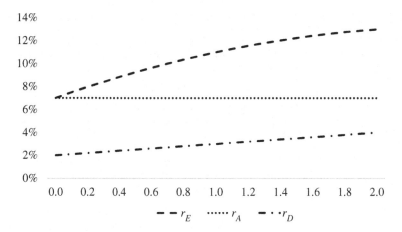

Figure 4.2 Leverage and cost of equity with increasing cost of debt.

assuming that the cost of debt gradually rises from 2 to 4 percent along with the increase in leverage. The result shows that the increase in the cost of equity is partly offset by a corresponding rise in the cost of debt. This also means that the expected rate of return for equity investors is lower when debt investors require a larger slice of the pie, resulting in a smaller slice left for the former.

Let us now introduce the corporate tax. The key effect of the tax is that of a **tax shield** on debt. The tax benefit arises because interest expenses are tax-deductible while equity-related costs, such as dividends, are not. Since the burden of the deduction is borne by the government in the form of reduced tax revenues, firms can enjoy the tax benefit without any offsetting effect. Broadly seen, though, reduced tax revenues for the public sector might lead to indirect consequences such as less reliable business infrastructure and less stimulus for consumption.

With the tax shield effect on debt, the WACC is expressed as follows:

$$r_{WACC} = r_D (1-t) \frac{V_D}{V_A} + r_E \frac{V_E}{V_A}$$

where r_{WACC} is the after-tax weighted average cost of capital and t is the corporate tax rate. Notice that the average cost of capital for a firm is lower than that under the assumption of no tax, to the extent that the cost of debt is lower by $(1 - t)$. This is the effect of the tax shield on WACC. When the after-tax WACC is applied to discount free cash flow in valuing a firm, the lower discount rate leads to a higher value, the difference being the value of the tax shield.

Figure 4.3 shows the effect of the tax shield on the cost of capital, by comparing the unlevered cost of capital (r_A) and the after-tax WACC (r_{WACC}). Although the difference seems graphically small, the effect on value is not. For instance, when the debt-to-equity ratio is 1.0, the cost of equity is $7\% + (7\% - 3\%) \times 1.0 = 11$ percent, assuming an unlevered cost of capital of 7 percent and a cost of debt of 3 percent under the leverage level. With a tax rate of 30 percent, the after-tax WACC is $3\% \times (1 - 30\%) \times (50/100) + 11\% \times (50/100) = 6.55$ percent. Although the difference from the unlevered cost of capital is just 0.45 percent, the effect on value is larger: When used as the discount rate of a perpetuity with a constant cash flow of 100, for instance, the value without the tax shield is $100/0.07 = 1,429$, while that with the tax shield increases to $100/0.0655 = 1,527$, a difference of 6.9 percent in value. Reflecting this difference, firms compete even for a difference in rate of 0.01 percent, or 1 basis point, in negotiating the cost of debt when issuing bonds.

In a world in which tax exists, a firm with debt generates additional financial value through the tax shield provided by debt. If a firm expects a constant flow of tax shields by keeping its debt amount constant, its annual interest expenses are $V_D \cdot r_D$, and the acquired tax shield is

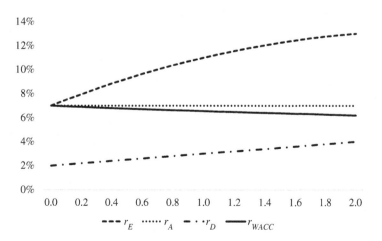

Figure 4.3 Leverage and weighted average cost of capital.

expressed as $V_D \cdot r_D \cdot t$. Assuming a perpetuity of annual tax shields with a discount rate of r_D, the present value of the tax shield of debt is $V_D \cdot r_D \cdot t / r_D = V_D \cdot t$. The result means that the use of debt in a firm's capital structure decisions increases the firm's value by the amount of $V_D \cdot t$, even if its business is unchanged. This increase is a correction of the original MM theorem, because financial decisions do affect a firm's value in the presence of tax. As explained, the source of the value is the transfer of value from the government in the form of reduced taxes. In summary, the result shows that while capital structure is irrelevant to firm value, it is relevant in the presence of tax to the extent that it affects the value of the tax shield on debt.

The reason why debt alone receives preferred treatment with regard to tax is mostly historical. Originating in 1918 as a temporary measure intended to equalize the effect of the excess profit tax introduced in the U.S. during World War I, the practice was retained even after the repeal of the excess profit tax in 1921.[4] Similar provisions are used in most countries today, but the difference in treatment has been shown to cause a distortion toward debt over equity.[5]

The value of the tax shield on debt tells us that higher leverage leads to higher firm value. The relationship is expressed as follows:

$$V_A = V_U + V_D t = V_D + V_E$$

where V_U is the value of the **unlevered firm**. When we think of a firm's balance sheet in terms of market value as in Figure 4.4, its whole assets, whose value is V_A, consist of the value of its operating assets, which equals V_U, and the value of the tax shield, which is V_{TX}. When a firm has no leverage, V_D and V_{TX} are zero, so $V_A = V_U = V_E$.

2.1. Tradeoff theory

If the value of the tax shield is proportional to leverage, the optimal capital structure would be the maximum level of leverage with an infinitesimal

---

[4]Warren, A. C. (1974). The corporate interest deduction: A policy evaluation. *Yale Law Journal*, 83(8), 1585–1619.
[5]Heider, F. and Ljungqvist, A. (2015). As certain as debt and taxes: Estimating the tax sensitivity of leverage from state tax changes. *Journal of Financial Economics*, 118(3), 684–712.

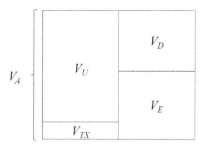

Figure 4.4   Market-value balance sheet with tax shield.

amount of equity. This is not intuitive, however, because in reality a firm risks bankruptcy if it takes on too much debt. When actually defaulting on its debt, it incurs various costs through court proceedings, where debt and equity investors try to recoup their investments. These costs include direct costs, such as fees for lawyers, accountants and consultants, as well as indirect ones such as damage to brand value and reputation, weaker demand from customers, and lower employee engagement and supplier commitment. Faced with these **financial distress costs**, a firm chooses an optimal capital structure where the marginal benefit of the tax shield equals the marginal cost of financial distress, as shown in Figure 4.5. Firm value that takes into consideration the financial distress cost is:

$$V_A = V_U + V_D t - \mathrm{PV(FDC)}$$

where PV(FDC) is the present value of the financial distress cost. Its value is the probability of default times the amount of costs incurred when the default occurs, which means that PV (FDC) = PV {(FDC | default) × (Probability of default)}. The **tradeoff theory** posits that a firm sets its optimal capital structure based on a tradeoff between the value of the tax shield on debt and the financial distress costs that accompany leverage. The theory was proposed by Modigliani and Miller as a correction to their original theorem, which assumed no tax.[6]

---

[6]Modigliani, F. and Miller, M. H. (1963). Corporate income taxes and the cost of capital: A correction. *American Economic Review*, 53(3), 433–443.

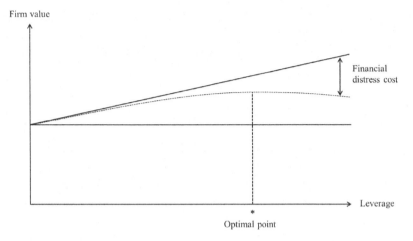

Firm value

Financial
distress cost

Leverage

*
Optimal point

Figure 4.5 Optimal capital structure.

3. Capital Structure and the Cost of Capital

The MM theorem enables us to analyze how the cost of equity is affected by changes in capital structure. Because firms adopt different capital structures, this is helpful in understanding risk and the required cost of equity.

The analysis is done in two stages: "unlevering" and "relevering." In the former, the unlevered cost of a firm's capital is obtained from its actual level of leverage. This cost is independent of capital structure as long as a firm's business is unchanged. In the latter stage, the required cost of equity is obtained from the unlevered cost of capital given a target capital structure. In the following, we see two models for this purpose with two assumptions: a firm's constant debt ratio, and a firm's constant amount of debt.

3.1. Constant debt ratio

The unlevered cost of capital corresponds to the risk of a firm's assets. By using the CAPM introduced in Chapter 1, the risk is expressed as a firm's **asset beta**, or **unlevered beta**, which indicates the risk of its entire assets regardless of capital structure. Using the asset beta, we can derive the required cost of capital that investors need to take on the risk. Under the MM theorem, we can view the risk of a firm's assets as a portfolio of debt and equity risks when its capital structure, indicated by the debt-to-asset ratio, is constant:

$$\beta_A = \beta_D \frac{V_D}{V_A} + \beta_E \frac{V_E}{V_A}$$

where β_A is the asset beta, β_D is the debt beta, and β_E is the equity beta of a firm. This is essentially the same expression as that for the unlevered cost of capital of a firm developed in the previous section, except that the cost of capital is replaced by a beta. Given a beta, a cost of capital such as r_A, r_D, and r_E is correspondingly determined by applying the CAPM. The assumption that the unlevered cost of capital is constant therefore means that the asset beta is, too, regardless of a firm's capital structure, as long as its underlying business risk is unchanged.

The equation above holds true with or without the presence of tax when we assume that the risk of the tax shield is equal to that of the operating assets. More specifically, in the presence of tax, the entire risk of a firm's assets is expressed as follows:

$$\beta_A = \beta_U \frac{V_U}{V_A} + \beta_{TX} \frac{V_{TX}}{V_A}$$

where β_U is the unlevered beta, β_{TX} is the tax shield beta of a firm, and V_U and V_{TX} are, respectively, the value of the unlevered firm and the tax shield. When we assume that β_{TX} is equal to β_U, that also means that β_U is equal to β_A because β_A is a portfolio of β_U and β_{TX}, as shown in Figure 4.4. The tax shield involves risk in that a firm is unable to enjoy it without sufficient taxable income, such as when it runs a deficit. Assuming that β_{TX} is equal to β_U means that the risk is approximated by the riskiness of the firm's business, which is expressed by β_U. Under this assumption, we do not need to treat the risk of the tax shield separately, and can focus on assessing the riskiness of the firm's operating assets. It also enables us to use the asset beta, β_A, and the unlevered beta, β_U, interchangeably; otherwise, the two are affected by the relative value and riskiness of the tax shield.[7]

---

[7]Miles, J. A. and Ezzel, J. R. (1980). The weighted average cost of capital, perfect capital markets and project life: A clarification. *Journal of Financial and Quantitative Analysis*, 15(3), 719–730.

Table 4.1   Unlevering and relevering.

Firm	Equity	Debt	β_E	β_D	β_A
A	80	20	1.2	0.1	0.98
B	150	150	1.6	0.2	0.90
C	200	100	1.4	0.1	0.97
Average					0.95
Target leverage (V_D/V_E)					0.2
β_D					0.1
β_E					1.12
Market risk premium					5%
Risk-free rate					2%
r_E					7.6%

Let us see how we can unlever firms in practice. Suppose that there are three listed firms, comparable to a target firm, whose risk we need to estimate. Table 4.1 shows a summary of the capital structure and beta of each firm. From the data we are able to compute the asset beta for each firm. For instance, by using the equation $\beta_A = \beta_D \times V_D/V_A + \beta_E \times V_E/V_A$, the asset beta of Firm A is calculated as $0.1 \times (20/100) + 1.2 \times (80/100) = 0.98$, given that the proportion of debt to assets, or V_D/V_A, is $20/100$ and that of equity to assets, or V_E/V_A, is $80/100$. Similarly, the asset betas of firms B and C are 0.90 and 0.97, respectively. By averaging these numbers, we obtain an estimate of the target firm's asset beta, which is 0.95.

While the above example includes only firms with positive debt value, the value can be negative if a firm has no debt and instead carries excess liquidity, meaning that it carries *negative* net debt. The same formula applies even in such a case, resulting in an asset beta that is *larger* than the equity beta. This is because an equity stake in a firm consists of a portfolio of a firm's operating assets and its liquidity. Since the liquidity part is essentially risk-free, an equity stake carries the risks of a portfolio of risky operating assets and risk-free assets. The equity beta of such a firm is lower than that of a firm without excess liquidity, even if both have the same business, because the former reflects the relative safety of including risk-free assets in its portfolio.

Using the estimated asset beta, we then relever the target firm. When the target leverage of the firm expressed by its debt-to-equity ratio (V_D/V_E)

is 0.2 and its debt beta is 0.10, the equity beta of the firm is calculated as $0.95 + (0.95 - 0.10) \times 0.2 = 1.12$ because the equation solved for β_E is $\beta_E = \beta_A + (\beta_A - \beta_D) \times V_D/V_E$. Additionally, when we assume a market risk premium of 5 percent and a risk-free rate of 2 percent under the CAPM, the required cost of equity is $1.12 \times 5\% + 2\% = 7.6$ percent.

3.2. Constant debt amount

Next, we see another model of the unlevering and relevering with a different assumption about capital structure and riskiness of debt. Suppose now that capital structure, measured by debt-to-asset ratio, is not constant, but the amount of debt is — such as when a firm with a matured debt continues to refinance it in the same amount — and the debt is risk-free. The former assumption may not be a good fit for growing firms, whose amount of debt grows as its balance sheet expands, but may work for mature firms. The latter assumption, while possibly not true for a highly levered firm, should be a reasonable one for firms that issue high-quality debt comparable to government bonds.

In this scenario, we have another formula for the unlevering and relevering:[8]

$$\beta_A = \frac{\beta_E}{1 + (1-t)\frac{V_D}{V_E}}$$

where t is the corporate tax rate of a firm.

Table 4.2 shows the result of applying the equation to firms comparable to those shown in Table 4.1. For the unlevering part, the asset beta of Firm A is calculated as $1.2/\{1 + (1 - 30\%) \times 20/80\} = 1.02$. The average for the three firms is 1.0, as shown in the table. For the relevering part, given the same target leverage of 0.2 expressed by debt-to-equity ratio, the equity beta is calculated as $1.0 \times \{1 + 0.2 \times (1 - 30\%)\} = 1.14$. This makes the required cost of equity $1.14 \times 5\% + 2\% = 7.7$ percent.

While it is appropriate to apply these formulae according to assumptions made about a firm's target leverage, it is worthwhile to note that these assumptions may not be precisely true in reality because a firm's

---

[8]Hamada, R. (1972). The effect of the firm's capital structure on the systematic risk of common stocks. *Journal of Finance*, 27(2), 435–452.

Table 4.2 Unlevering and relevering under different assumptions.

Firm	Equity	Debt	β_E	β_A
A	80	20	1.2	1.02
B	150	150	1.6	0.94
C	200	100	1.4	1.04
Average				1.00
Target leverage (V_D/V_E)				0.2
Tax rate				30%
β_E				1.14
Market risk premium				5%
Risk-free rate				2%
r_E				7.7%

capital structure undergoes constant change. The market value of a firm's equity undergoes continual change in the financial markets. But rather than dynamically reacting to each change, firms are most likely to adjust their capital structure discretely, by means such as issuing and redeeming debt securities or issuing and repurchasing shares from time to time. Firms may also opportunistically exploit the relative attractiveness of issuing certain financial instruments in the financial markets, even if it makes them temporarily deviate from their leverage target. Because firms are likely to meander within their target boundaries of leverage, it is safe to say that the assumptions hold valid only in the long run.[9]

4. Capital Structure Under Conflicts of Interest

Alternative theories exist to explain a firm's capital structure. These are based on the **asymmetric information** and **conflicts of interest** between firms and investors — factors which are absent in the MM theorem, which assumes perfect information and no transaction costs when the capital structure is established. First we look at the pecking order theory, which derives from the asymmetric information discussed in the previous

[9]Marsh, P. (1982). The choice between equity and debt: An empirical study. *Journal of Finance*, 37(1), 121–144.

chapter. Next, by examining conflicts of interest between managers and shareholders, we see how the agency theory works in setting capital structure.

4.1. Pecking order theory

The **pecking order theory** originates in the idea that there is a difference in information, or asymmetric information,[10] between firms and investors.[11] Under the MM theorem's assumption of perfect information and no transaction cost, a firm can finance a project whenever it likes at a price that appropriately reflects the information it has at the time of financing. As discussed in the previous chapter, however, firms are likely to have more information than investors because of proprietary information, such as trade secrets, which they keep within their boundaries.

In this case, firms, being aware of investors' relative lack of information, may become reluctant to issue securities out of fear of being undervalued. Investors, meanwhile, equally aware that they are less informed, may become reluctant to invest if they conclude that firms will issue securities only when believing themselves overvalued. In addition, there are the costs entailed in issuing securities in the real financial markets, such as fees paid to investment banks and lawyers and the time required to complete financing transactions. In this situation, firms choose to look for other sources of capital before ever seeking financing from investors outside their corporate boundaries.

These motives lead firms to choose internal financing, drawing on part of the earnings that remain after paying out dividends and repurchasing shares. Depreciation and amortization of assets also play a part in internal financing, because these are non-cash expenses in calculating earnings, meaning that the cash equivalent for the depreciated and amortized amounts remains within firms even if expensed.

Even when firms must deploy external financing, they first turn to debt financing rather than equity. The former is less information-intensive, in that conditions such as maturity and rate of return are

---

[10]Akerlof, G. A. (1970). The market for "lemons": Quality uncertainty and the market mechanism. *Quarterly Journal of Economics*, 84(3), 488–500.

[11]Myers, S. C. and Majluf, N. S. (1984). Corporate financing and investment decisions when firms have information that investors do not have. *Journal of Financial Economics*, 13(2), 187–221.

contractually set at the beginning, the probability of default is learned by checking credit ratings based on past statistics, and failure to repay can lead to court proceedings. Transaction costs, such as underwriting fees, are also lower than those required for equity financing.

In contrast, equity financing involves a greater information gap than debt financing because its valuation is more dependent on uncertain future prospects which lack statistical backing. Also, the contractual protection provided to investors in terms of cash flow certainty is weaker than that provided by debt, since shareholders are promised no payouts beforehand; even when a firm fails to realize the financial prospects it might share at the time of issuance, contractual consequences are not invoked. These properties widen the degree of asymmetric information. Fees are also higher for equity financing, and transactions take longer to complete, meaning that more managerial resources are consumed. These differences result in a "pecking order" of funds, with internal funds being the most preferred, followed by debt and finally by equity. The pecking order theory explains the effects of asymmetric information and transaction costs that exist when firms design capital structure in the real world.

The theory also explains actual corporate decisions from a different perspective to that of the tradeoff theory. Firms will often have some of the characteristics predicted by both theories simultaneously.[12] Well-performing firms tend to have a low level of debt in the first place. This contradicts the tradeoff theory in that financial distress costs are low for these firms, which are supposed to use their debt capacity to best increase the value of the tax shield. The pecking order theory, in contrast, has no trouble explaining this as it is the result of firms' choosing internal over external funds when they are able to do so.

Secondly, companies with a high level of fixed tangible assets, such as utility and real estate firms, tend to have higher leverage, while those that rely on intangible assets, such as high-tech or pharmaceutical companies reliant on human capital and research and development, tend to have lower leverage. The tradeoff theory explains this as the result of differences in financial distress costs. The former group has more assets that can be utilized as collateral for debt financing, thus lowering the financial distress cost, while the latter group's assets are mostly intangible, meaning that bankruptcy will result in the loss of a significant part of their sources

---

[12]Rajan, R. G. and Zingales, L. (1995). What do we know about capital structure? Some evidence from international data. *Journal of Finance*, 50(5), 1421–1460.

of value, such as employees' skills and ideas. The pecking order theory explains this as the result of differences in the information held by firms and investors. The former group has more visible assets and a smaller information gap, while the latter has less visible assets and greater uncertainty in business and valuation, resulting in a preference for using internal funds to avoid unfavorable consequences. Maintaining a low level of leverage also gives such firms the **financial flexibility** to deal with uncertainty in the course of their business.

Both theories have a sound foundation, but neither seems complete on its own; rather, they give complementary explanations of capital structure decisions. Firms are not homogeneous, either, in that each makes its own capital structure decisions based on individual market positions and preferences. They may have, for instance, different outlooks on their future performance, which relate to differing estimates of financial distress cost, appetite for risk, and self-valuation in the financial markets. These differences cause variations in capital structure, even among firms in similar businesses.

4.2. Agency theory

Capital structure is also affected by the different incentives of managers and shareholders. Under the **separation of ownership and control**, managers may have an incentive to benefit and entrench themselves at the expense of shareholders. This is the **agency problem** discussed in the previous chapter.[13] From this perspective, the **free cash flow hypothesis** posits that if a firm's leverage is high enough to absorb excess free cash flow that managers would otherwise be tempted to spend for unproductive purposes, such as empire-building or extravagant perks, its capital structure can have a **disciplinary effect**.[14] The choice of high leverage thus sends a signal that the firm's managers are willing to run a tight ship and avoid defaulting on debt, and thereby mitigates the agency problem

---

[13] Jensen, M. C. and Meckling, W. H. (1976). Theory of the firm: Managerial behavior, agency costs and ownership structure. *Journal of Financial Economics*, 3(4), 305–360.

[14] Jensen, M. C. (1986). Agency costs of free cash flow, corporate finance, and takeovers. *American Economic Review*, 76(2), 323–329; Jensen, M. C. (1989). The eclipse of the public corporation. *Harvard Business Review*, 67(5), 61–74.

between shareholders and managers.[15] Debt may even have such an effect vis-à-vis employees, as the use of high leverage sends a signal within the firm that its managers are determined to run things efficiently and get rid of slack.[16]

In the case of a **leveraged buyout (LBO)**, where a firm takes on a significantly high level of debt and works on raising operating efficiency for improved shareholder value, the firm has little choice but to repay that debt from its cash flow. Where shareholders, such as private equity funds, have control over capital structure decisions, they may prefer such a disciplinary effect. While high leverage means that a firm will enjoy a large tax shield, as the tradeoff theory explains, the agency theory offers a different perspective in the added benefit of the disciplinary effect on managers under the separation of ownership and control.

Of course, high leverage is not free from the financial distress costs predicated by the tradeoff theory, as highly leveraged firms may go bankrupt by failing to meet the level of free cash flow required to repay their debts. Examples include bankruptcies by the energy conglomerate TXU Corporation in 2013 and Toys 'R' Us in 2017, as well as J.Crew and Hertz in 2020 amid the pandemic. However, it has been shown that firms overall enjoy improved performance with the involvement of private equity funds.[17] The free cash flow hypothesis gave theoretical support to a surge in LBO transactions in the 1980s and the following decades.

5. Debt–Shareholders Conflict

Finally, we analyze the effects of capital structure in **conflicts of interest** between debtholders and shareholders. While debtholders have seniority over shareholders in the recovery of their investments, shareholders have an unlimited upside in the return received after repayment to debtholders. The difference in their respective financial payoffs creates an incentive for one side to harm the other. When we consider this incentive, the effect of high leverage is more nuanced, particularly in extreme cases, because it

---

[15] Jensen, M. C. (1986). Agency costs of free cash flow, corporate finance, and takeovers. *American Economic Review*, 76(2), 323–329.

[16] Wruck, K. H. (1995). Financial policy as a catalyst for organizational change: Sealed Air's leveraged special dividend. *Journal of Applied Corporate Finance*, 7(4), 20–35.

[17] Kaplan, S. N. and Stromberg, P. (2009). Leveraged buyouts and private equity. *Journal of Economic Perspectives*, 23(1), 121–146.

induces behaviors that do not satisfy everyone. On the one hand, it may induce excessive risk taking, counter to the intended disciplinary effect. On the other, it may induce underinvestment beyond the intended effect of preventing empire-building. We shall see these effects, the **asset substitution problem** and the **debt overhang problem**, in the following. They are also manifestations of the moral hazards discussed in the previous chapter, in that the conflicts arise post-transaction when one party cannot fully monitor the other.

5.1. Asset substitution problem

The **asset substitution problem** is an example of conflicts that arise between debtholders and shareholders in a highly leveraged situation.[18] This occurs when shareholders try to increase the value of their holdings at the expense of debtholders. Using the option theory, one can view equity as a long position of a **call option**, with corporate assets as underlying assets and the face value of debt as the exercise price. Similarly, one can view debt as a composite of the face value of debt and a short position of a **put option**, with the same underlying assets and exercise price.[19] As shown in Figure 4.6, this means the payoffs are asymmetrical: Shareholders enjoy unlimited gains with an increase in a firm's asset value, while the downside is mitigated by **limited liability**. Limited liability means that even if the value of a firm's assets falls below that of its debt, the firm does not have to compensate for the loss once it gives up its stake, and debtholders assume the remaining loss. Debtholders, meanwhile, gain nothing beyond face value, while a decrease in asset value causes them loss.

As long as a firm is operating or growing with stability, neither type of investor has a problem. Debtholders receive their promised repayments on schedule, and shareholders enjoy a stream of dividends and increases in the value of their holdings as capital gains. It is when a firm approaches bankruptcy, in the sense that the market value of its assets nears the face

---

[18] Jensen, M. C. and Meckling, W. H. (1976). Theory of the firm: Managerial behavior, agency costs and ownership structure. *Journal of Financial Economics*, 3(4), 305–360; Leland, H. E. (1998). Agency costs, risk management, and capital structure. *Journal of Finance*, 53(4), 1213–1243.

[19] Merton, R. C. (1974). On the pricing of corporate debt: The risk structure of interest rates. *Journal of Finance*, 29(2), 449–470.

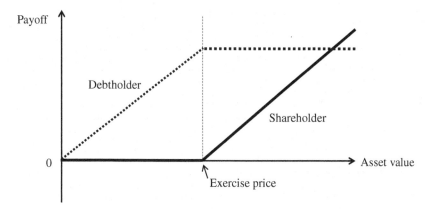

Figure 4.6 Shareholder and debtholder positions.

value of its debt or even falls below it, that the differing interests of shareholders and debtholders become apparent. At that time, with the value of equity close to zero, shareholders have nothing more to lose under the protection of limited liability. But if a risky project arises that will substantially improve cash flow or further widen losses, shareholders will have an incentive to undertake it, as it can only result in their gain. This is consistent with their option position, which increases in value with the volatility of underlying assets through the risky undertaking.

In contrast, debtholders are sure to widen the loss of their position if the project fails, while gaining little even if it succeeds, because the upper limit of the value of their holdings is bound by the face value of their debt. The upside belongs only to shareholders, which gives debtholders the opposite incentive of rejecting the project. This is also consistent with their option position, which decreases in value with the volatility of underlying assets. This asymmetry in payoff, viewed as opposing option positions, creates a conflict between shareholders and debtholders over investment decisions. When debtholders cannot monitor shareholders, managers may undertake risky projects in accord with the shareholders' preferences.

Let us look at one example. Table 4.3 shows a situation in which debtholders and shareholders have stakes in a firm. Suppose the face value of the firm's debt is 100, but its asset value is lower at 80. There is a risky project that would either lift the asset value of the firm to 180 with a 50 percent probability or lower it to 20 otherwise. The firm should be

Table 4.3 Asset substitution problem.

	Before	After		Expected value
		Success (50%)	Failure (50%)	
Asset value	80	180	20	100
Debt value	80	100	20	60
Equity value	0	80	0	40

better off undertaking the project, because the expected value of its assets would increase from 80 to 100 as a whole. However, debtholders want to reject the project because a decrease in the expected value of debt from 80 to 60 would widen their loss. Shareholders want to undertake the project because the expected value of equity would improve from 0 to 40. This improvement would derive not only from the increase in asset value, which would increase from 80 to 100, but also from the decrease in debt value, which would fall from 80 to 60.

This can mean that shareholder value is created not only by undertaking projects with a positive net present value, but also by transferring value from debtholders to shareholders. This occurs because their positions have opposite constructions. An increase in value for shareholders means an equivalent decrease in value for debtholders.

Should debtholders demand a higher interest rate in anticipation of this potential transfer of value as compensation for any expected loss, it is shareholders who will ultimately bear the brunt of the higher borrowing costs that result. This occurs even if shareholders have no actual intention to harm debtholders but do have the incentive and ability to do so afterward, unless they can give debtholders credible assurance that they will not do so.

This is a form of *information cost*, a cost that arises from the existence of asymmetric information between the two sides. Because the information cost is ultimately borne by shareholders themselves, it is in their interest to lower it. Debt covenants mitigate this problem by limiting investment by firms or subjecting it to debtholders' approval in advance. Bankruptcy codes also allow debtholders, as well as firms, to file petitions. This gives debtholders legal protection by entitling them to court intervention in preventing the value of their holdings from deteriorating further. It also gives them bargaining power against shareholders in such situations.

5.2. Debt overhang problem

Another type of conflict between debtholders and shareholders is the **debt overhang problem**.[20] This arises when firms with excessive debt are unable to undertake profitable projects because of opposition by both debtholders and shareholders. It occurs when firms are already burdened with excessive debt and in financial constraints. On the one hand, debtholders are reluctant to lend additional money when the value of their existing holdings is already below its face value, and additional lending could further increase their losses by throwing good money after bad. On the other hand, shareholders, too, are reluctant to invest because it is debtholders who would benefit from any improvement in corporate value arising from the project's success. If the additional value will go to debtholders, even when the initial investment has been made by shareholders, the latter will see the new investment as a value-destroying proposition.

Let us look at another example in Table 4.4. Suppose that a new investment project has a moderate risk, and will lift asset value with a 50 percent probability but will keep it unchanged otherwise. It requires an initial investment of 10, which is not listed in the table because it is uncertain whether it will be paid by debtholders or shareholders. The project increases the firm's asset value to either 140 or 80, raising its expected value from 80 to 110. This means that the expected value of debt also increases from 80 to 90. However, let us further suppose that debtholders cannot lend additional money to this project, even if it proves lucrative, because their holdings, with a value of 80, have already incurred a loss of 20 against their face value of 100, and that they are restricted from additional lending which could further deteriorate the value of their existing holdings.

Table 4.4   Debt overhang problem.

	Before	After		
		Success (50%)	Failure (50%)	Expected value
Asset value	80	140	80	110
Debt value	80	100	80	90
Equity value	0	40	0	20

---

[20]Myers, S. C. (1977). Determinants of corporate borrowing. *Journal of Financial Economics*, 5(2), 147–175.

If we look at the payoff for shareholders of the additional investment of 10, we see the net present value is 10, improving the expected value of equity from 0 to 20 with the additional investment. Shareholders, however, are also reluctant to invest in this project because the investment will benefit not themselves but debtholders, who will see a windfall improvement in the value of their holdings from 80 to 90 thanks to the additional risk-taking by shareholders. This occurs because of the difficulty of having both sides to clarify future events and agree on the distribution of value beforehand.

In sum, conflicts between shareholders and debtholders can even result in the rejection of a project with a positive net present value. In the sense that the rejected project might have raised the asset value of the firm as a whole, it could also mean that socially desirable projects that add value are rejected.

5.2.1. Project finance

One avenue for solving this problem is the use of **project finance**. This is a financing structure based on a contractual arrangement under which a firm establishes a separate vehicle as a sponsor which is legally remote from its bankruptcy. The vehicle, a **special purpose vehicle (SPV)**, raises capital through new equity and debt investments based solely on the prospects of the project it undertakes on the basis of its own decisions on optimal capital structure.[21] Such a capital structure may also be different from the sponsor's. The separate structure of this entity means that debtholders of existing sponsor firms do not need to worry about any further deterioration to their existing holdings. They may even be willing to lend to the SPV. Similarly, shareholders, even if they invest in the SPV, need not worry about a transfer of value to existing debtholders, because new debt is raised on a clean slate based solely on the project's value.

However, not all projects are suitable for a project finance arrangement. First, the entity needs to operate independently from its sponsor parent firms, and cash flow from the project must also be treated independently. If a manufacturer of widgets establishes an SPV to create a similar widget, that will not make sense because the performance of the SPV

---

[21] Leland, H. E. (2007). Financial synergies and the optimal scope of the firm: Implications for mergers, spinoffs, and structured finance. *Journal of Finance*, 62(2), 765–807.

depends largely on the capability of the sponsor firm and is not remote from its bankruptcy. Infrastructure and real estate development projects, for instance, are suitable from this perspective, because their assets have their own value separate from any sponsor firms. In emerging economies, infrastructure projects in fields such as energy, transportation, and telecommunications are often funded through project finance because it allows those countries to raise capital independently of their sovereign credit ratings.

6. Conclusion

Because of the many different forces in play, the optimal capital structure can be elusive. It is helpful, therefore, to put the various theories in perspective. Taking as a point of departure the irrelevance theorem and the tradeoff theory proposed by Modigliani and Miller in the 1950s and 1960s, which predict that firms will tread a path that balances tax benefits and financial distress costs for an optimal structure, the development of theories on capital structure has added various perspectives by incorporating relevant theories appearing in the field of economics. The primary example is the pecking order theory, which incorporates the concept of asymmetric information formalized in the 1970s by Akerlof into decisions on capital structure. This development was followed by efforts to incorporate the agency theory, established in the same decade by Jensen and Meckling, into such decisions, shedding a new light on conflicts of interest between managers and investors as well as between debtholders and shareholders.

The influence of the original MM theorem has been so enormous that it remains the fundamental framework for capital structure. Practitioners still rely on its basic concept in assessing the required costs of capital for firms in the financial markets through the unlevering and relevering processes. It has also affected thinking on the perennial issue of the relationship between firms and investors by promoting a better understanding of the incentives of each. Theories developed in the past decades have further affected contractual practices in financing, including LBOs and project finance, enabling firms and investors to benefit from financial arrangements under information asymmetry and conflicts of interest with better predictability and protection. The MM theorem, along with subsequent developments, has provided firms with a standard to refer to when making decisions on capital structure.

Chapter 5

Merging and Acquiring Businesses

1. Overview

Mergers and acquisitions (M&A) are one of the strategies by which firms pursue growth. Firms may also choose to divest some of their businesses to refocus on a core domain. Managers seeking an acquisition may put anti-takeover defenses in place to provide against a hostile takeover attempt. Mergers and acquisitions, or **business combinations**, are a complex field of financial management, lying as they do at the crossroads of strategic, financial, and legal perspectives. Their impact on growth is significant in that they bring discontinuous changes to a firm's trajectories. This chapter deals with the structures and economics of mergers and acquisitions, and offers some legal viewpoints from which to execute these transactions.

1.1. Synergy

One of the major objectives of a merger or acquisition is to create **synergy**. Synergy is the economic gains generated through a business combination that make the value of the combined business greater than the sum of its parts. For example, a combined business can produce sales of goods and services that are larger than the sum of the sales of its constituent businesses, as the combined business has expanded access to sales networks as well as marketing know-how in different customer and geographic segments. A combination can develop new goods and services by blending the ideas and technologies of each component firm. It can also lower costs and raise profit margins by eliminating duplicate functions and facilities, while benefiting from increased bargaining power with suppliers. Economic gains like these are calculated before a transaction is agreed upon, and are an important justification for mergers and acquisitions.

In contrast, a business **divestiture** takes place when a firm sells, or spins off, a part of its business. Similar to the motive for mergers and acquisitions, a major objective of a divestiture is to create economic gains by unwinding a business combination so that the sum of the parts can produce more value than the original combined firm. Through divestiture, managers can give each business its proper focus, rather than being distracted by running a combination of several different businesses. Investors, too, may give greater value to individual firms that clearly represent an industry or segment than to a bundle of different businesses with complicated relationships, as a divestiture will allow them to easily diversify their investments in the public markets. In a divestiture, the seller firm receives payment for a divested business while focusing on the business or businesses that remain. If the total value is greater than the value of the combined business, the transaction adds value in total.

Since most merger and acquisition transactions require a buyer and a seller, they need to satisfy two conditions simultaneously: a purchase must create synergy for the buyer, and a mirroring sale must create synergy for the seller. The buyer may be an industry player endeavoring to strengthen its market position or diversify its business, or a private equity fund aiming to operate the acquired firm and resell it in several years. The acquisition target may be a competing firm in the same industry, or one of the portfolio companies of a private equity or venture capital fund looking to exit its investment.

For a buyer seeking an acquisition, it is necessary to satisfy the following condition:

$$V_{AT} \geq V_A + V_T$$

where V_A is the value of the acquirer firm, V_T is the value of the target firm, and V_{AT} is the value of the combined businesses.

For a seller wishing to divest, it is necessary to satisfy the opposite condition:

$$V_X + V_T \geq V_{XT}$$

where V_X is the value of the divesting firm, V_T is the value of the divested firm, and V_{XT} is the value of the combined businesses. A divested firm is a target firm from the viewpoint of an acquirer. When a divesting firm is a private equity or venture capital fund, a higher value means that the divestiture realizes capital gain by separating a portfolio company from the capital pool that has added to its value since its original investment.

1.2. Enforcement of competition law

A business combination may improve value as a result of market concentration as well. There is concern, for instance, that U.S. digital platform firms such as Google and Facebook exercise excessive market power to the detriment of consumers and suppliers, while nipping in the bud those startups that could threaten them in the near future.[1] These giants are gathering increasing attention from regulators which accuse them of distorting competition.[2] Here the source of value lies in the excess earning power gained by having a monopolistic position amid undermined competition. Thus, despite the added economic value promised by business combinations, **competition laws** are used across the world to regulate the concentration of market power.

To measure market concentration, it is traditional for authorities to refer to the **Herfindahl–Hirschman Index (HHI)**, which is the sum of the squares of the shares, in percentage, of all firms in an industry. If only one firm operates in an industry, the index is 10,000, which is the square of 100. If 10 firms with a 10 percent share each operate in an industry, the index is 1,000, which is the sum of the square of 10 for ten firms. The index comes close to zero in a state of perfect competition, where the share of each competitor is minimal. The U.S. competition authority considers a market in which the index is between 1,500 and 2,500 points to be moderately concentrated, and one in which it exceeds 2,500 to be highly concentrated.[3] To mitigate market concentration, the authorities can block a deal or require a firm to divest some of its businesses as a condition for approving a proposed merger or acquisition. Such government-level

[1] Kamepalli, S. K., Rajan, R., and Zingales, L. (2020). Kill zone. NBER Working Paper, No. 27146.
[2] The U.S. Federal Trade Commission (2020). FTC sues Facebook for illegal monopolization, December 9, 2020; The U.S. Department of Justice (2020). Justice Department sues monopolist Google for violating antitrust laws, October 20, 2020.
[3] The Anti-Trust Division, The U.S. Department of Justice (2018). Herfindahl-Hirschman Index, July 31, 2018.

reviews are a far from negligible part of business combinations. While countries differ in the degree to which competition laws are enforced,[4] reviews made by the U.S., EU, and Chinese authorities for their own markets are usually important in obtaining global clearance for a transaction. The recent attention given to technology firms shows that post-merger market practices matter as well.

While such reviews are limited to the firm level, it has recently been suggested that a high degree of ownership by the same shareholders of different firms tends to undermine competition among them. This problem, which was first suggested during research into the U.S. airline industry,[5] is called the **common ownership** problem. It looks at concentration at the level of shareholders in an industry as opposed to that of firms. Specifically, the research shows that ownership concentration occurring as a result of a surge in passive investments by index funds, such as BlackRock, Vanguard, and State Street Global Advisors, reduces the incentive of airliners to compete against each other and leads to a rise in ticket prices. While this viewpoint does not find its way into formal reviews by authorities, it cautions against the negative effects that concentrated ownership can have on competitive markets.

1.3. Distribution of synergy

Let us see how synergy is distributed in the case of acquisition shown in Figure 5.1. Suppose that two firms combine their businesses and the acquirer firm pays a price, P_T, for the target firm. The gross synergy created by the acquisition is $V_{AT} - (V_A + V_T)$, and the acquirer decides to proceed only if the value is positive. However, the acquirer cannot obtain all of the benefits because the target firm and its shareholders demand a share in the form of a **premium**, which is expressed as $(P_T - V_T)$. The premium is typically around 20–40 percent of the market value of a target firm before a transaction is announced, but it can differ considerably depending on the **bargaining power** of each side of the transaction and general market conditions.

---

[4]Bradford, A. and Chilton, A. S. (2018). Competition law around the world from 1889 to 2010: The competition law index. *Journal of Competition Law & Economics*, 14(3), 393–432.

[5]Azar, J., Schmalz, M. C., and Tecu, I. (2018). Anticompetitive effects of common ownership. *Journal of Finance*, 73(4), 1513–1565.

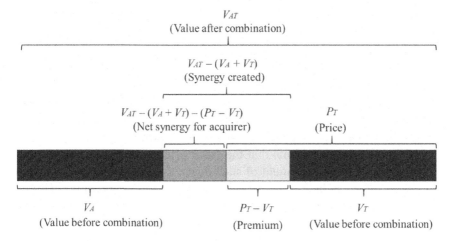

Figure 5.1 Synergy and distribution.

The premium cannot exceed the value of gross synergy created, because otherwise the net benefit for the acquirer becomes negative and incurs a loss for its shareholders. The net synergy for the acquirer, after sharing part of the synergy with the target firm, is $V_{AT} - (V_A + V_T) - (P_T - V_T)$. For the acquirer to proceed, this value needs to be positive.

It is worth noting that the synergy is the expected, and not the realized, value at the time of a transaction's closing, and therefore represents an uncertainty for the acquirer. In contrast, the premium is certain for the target firm, particularly when payment is made in cash. The acquirer breaks even when it realizes synergy equal to the premium paid, and enjoys net synergy only when it exceeds the threshold. It can happen, therefore, that an acquirer increases the value of a target firm but suffers a loss nevertheless, because of the high level of premium it has paid relative to the value added.

The stock market generally has a cautious attitude toward acquirers. It is known that on average, the stock price of an acquirer tends to fall when it announces a deal.[6] Research on U.S. deals made between 1980 and 2005 finds that the stock price of an acquirer rises on average

---

[6]Moeller, S. B., Schlingemann, F. P., and Stulz, R. M. (2005). Wealth destruction on a massive scale? A study of acquiring-firm returns in the recent merger wave. *Journal of Finance*, 60(2), 757–782.

by a mere 1 percent, and in half of deals it falls. In contrast, the stock price of a target firm rises on average by 15 percent; this reflects the premium that shareholders expect to receive, which averages 43 percent of the transaction value.[7] These results indicate two things: that it is harder for the managers of an acquirer to realize synergy than is apparent at the outset, at least at the level which justifies a premium, and that target firms are operated more efficiently than acquirers believe, leaving little room to raise value when they themselves sit behind the wheel.

Other research confirms that the stock prices of divesting firms tend to rise after the announcement of such deals; this holds true for all forms of divestitures, including stock sales, spin-offs, and carveouts.[8] This is consistent with the fact that sellers receive a premium at the time of a divestiture while buyers face uncertain success in their acquisitions.

The positive return for divesting firms also supports the notion that a divestiture unwinds a **conglomerate discount**, which is the discount on the stock price of a diversified firm. Such discounts were found mostly in the 1990s,[9] after a wave of diversifying acquisitions made by U.S. firms in the previous decade. They can occur when a firm lacks focus, operating multiple lines of businesses and letting inefficient businesses survive thanks to internal cross-subsidization. A conglomerate discount may not be universal, however, as research since the turn of the century reveals a conglomerate *premium*.[10] This essentially supports the original idea behind the diversifying acquisitions of the 1980s, that it was possible to increase value while decreasing risk. It has also been found that diversified firms performed better than stand-alones during the COVID-19 pandemic, when conglomerates were active in both highly affected industries

---

[7]Betton, S., Eckbo, B. E., and Thorburn, K. S. (2008). Corporate takeovers. In B. E. Eckbo (ed.), *Handbook of Corporate Finance: Empirical Corporate Finance*, *Vol. 2*. Amsterdam, The Netherlands: Elsevier/North-Holland, pp. 291–430.

[8]Eckbo, B. E. and Thornburn, K. S. (2013). Corporate restructuring. *Foundations and Trends in Finance*, 7(3), 159–288.

[9]Lang, L. H. P. and Stulz, R. M. (1994). Tobin's q, corporate diversification, and firm value. *Journal of Political Economy*, 102(6), 1248–1280; Berger, P. G. and Ofek, E. (1995). Diversification's effect on firm value. *Journal of Financial Economics*, 37(1), 39–65.

[10]Villalonga, B. (2004). Diversification discount or premium? New evidence from the Business Information Tracking Series. *Journal of Finance*, 51(2), 479–506.

and less affected ones.[11] The overall market response, however, shows that investors tend to be cautious about acquisitions while receptive to divestitures.

2. Choice of Payment

Buyers and sellers assume different types of risk according to how they choose to pay for a target firm. Payment in cash means that the acquirer takes on all risk relating to the performance of the target firm after its acquisition. In contrast, payment in stock means that the seller shares the risk in that the performance of the combined businesses is reflected in the value of the stock received in exchange. Another common method is to combine the two, in which case the seller takes both cash and stock.

This **choice of payment** is affected by tax considerations as well. Typically, sellers paying in cash become immediately liable for capital gains taxes when the acquisition price exceeds the tax base of their holdings, which is usually the price they originally paid. However, the use of stock for payment can defer capital gains taxes until the stock is sold in the future. Because of this difference, shareholders often prefer a stock payment for a tax-free transaction. Mixed payments of both stock and cash are often carefully structured in relation to applicable tax codes so as not to incur tax liabilities for the sellers. A majority of the payment may be made in stock, for example, so that the transaction is deemed equivalent to payment in stock as a whole.

The effects of payment choice are shown in Table 5.1. Suppose that an acquirer generates earnings of $100 million, and its stock is traded at $10 per share. The corporate tax rate for the firm is 30 percent. As it has no debt, and 100 million shares outstanding, the market capitalization of the stock is ($10 × 100 million) = $1 billion. The firm's earnings per share (EPS) are $1.00, which is $100 million/100 million shares, and its price-to-earnings ratio (PER) is 10, which is $10/$1.00.

The firm plans to acquire another firm. To focus on an analysis of the differing effects of payment choice, we assume that the target firm has the same financial characteristics as the acquirer in terms of market

---

[11] Fahlenbrach, R., Rageth, K., and Stultz, R. M. (2021). How valuable is financial flexibility when revenues stop? Evidence from the COVID-19 crisis. *Review of Financial Studies,* 34(11), pp. 5474–5521.

Table 5.1 Choice of payment.

	Acquirer	Target	Combined Cash	Combined Stock
Enterprise value	$1 bil.	$1 bil.	$2 bil.	$2 bil.
Debt value	—	—	$1 bil.	—
Equity value	$1 bil.	$1 bil.	$1 bil.	$2 bil.
Earnings	$100 mil.	$100 mil.	$179 mil.	$200 mil.
No. of shares	100 mil.	100 mil.	100 mil.	200 mil.
EPS	$1.00	$1.00	$1.79	$1.00
PER	10.0	10.0	5.6	10.0
Share price	$10	$10	$10	$10

capitalization, earnings, and number of shares outstanding. For simplicity, we further assume that the benefit of a tax shield through debt matches the cost of financial distress, thus neutralizing the effect.

2.1. Cash payment

When the acquirer chooses to pay in cash by issuing debt, the cost of which is 3 percent annually, it decreases the firm's EPS by $1 billion × 3% × (1 − 30%)/100 million, or $0.21 per share. The downward effect is similar when the firm uses its excess cash rather than issuing debt because it loses interest on the cash, though typically this is less than the debt cost. The acquisition lifts the firm's EPS by $1.00 per share by adding the performance of the target firm to that of the acquirer, resulting in a net value of ($1.00 − $0.21 + $1.00) = $1.79 per share.

However, the equity of the combined firm becomes financially riskier with an increase in leverage of $1 billion. Its credit rating is likely to fall as well, as reflected in the debt cost. The market value of the combined firm is now $2 billion. This reflects the free cash flow of the two firms, which is not affected by the choice of financing except for the tax shield and financial distress effects. The equity value remains at $1 billion, the difference obtained by subtracting the value of debt, $1 billion, from the enterprise value of $2 billion. The share price therefore remains unchanged at $10, which is $1 billion/100 million shares. The firm's PER, however, falls from 10 to 5.6, which is $1 billion/$179 million, reflecting the higher risk of the levered firm notwithstanding the higher EPS resulting from the combination.

The result of a lower PER can also be understood by seeing stock price as the value of a perpetuity. When all earnings are paid out as dividends, stock price is expressed as $EPS/(r - g)$ because dividends per share equal EPS, where r is the discount rate and g is the growth rate for the cash flow. Since PER is obtained by dividing the stock price by EPS, it is expressed as $1/(r - g)$. This result shows that PER is a function of risk indicated by r and growth potential indicated by g. Even if an acquisition raises the EPS, a higher leverage increases r as well, resulting in a lower PER.

2.2. Stock payment

If the acquirer chooses to pay in stock, it issues 100 million additional shares in a stock-for-stock deal, exchanging its stock worth \$10 with the target's worth \$10. In this case, the combined firm's EPS is unchanged at \$10, reflecting a market value of equity of (\$1 + \$1) = \$2 billion and a number of shares outstanding of (100 + 100) = 200 million. The combined firm has doubled its assets and earnings, and its equity base as well, resulting in the same share price and EPS.

The exchange ratio for a stock-for-stock acquisition is 1:1 in this example under an assumption of no premium. The ratio is a scale of the relative value and bargaining power of the two firms. If we relax the assumption and assume instead that the acquirer pays a premium, it will issue more shares for a higher exchange ratio. This leads to a lower EPS and stock price because the acquirer's shareholders are entitled to a smaller slice of the pie, other things being equal, with more shares outstanding. In such a case, the acquirer must create synergy to justify a higher exchange ratio, lest the transaction incurs a loss for its shareholders. Therefore, a higher premium raises the bar for expected synergy, something which shareholders generally view with caution.

As part of the payment conditions, the parties agree on either a fixed or floating exchange ratio. A fixed ratio means that the seller's shareholders receive a fixed number of shares of the acquirer's stock regardless of its price, and thus take the risk of a price fluctuation between the deal's agreement and its closing. A floating ratio makes shareholders immune to price fluctuations, as the exchange rate is adjusted according to such fluctuations and the amount of payment they receive is fixed.

2.3. *Summary*

The different effects of payment choice show that the choice is affected by the acquirer's debt capacity and expected financial performance as well as the willingness of the target's shareholders to take on risk after the transaction. Should an acquirer prefer a higher EPS and have a large unused debt capacity that it can deploy without overly affecting its financial risk, it makes sense for it to pay in cash by issuing debt. If it has little debt capacity, it would make more sense to pay in stock. Issuing additional shares for an acquisition, however, causes dilution per se, and the impact on the buyer's EPS and stock price depends on the value added by the transaction relative to the increase in the number of shares outstanding. Any additional premium leads to a further dilution, resulting in lower EPS and stock price, other things being equal. Negotiating the premium is critical as it affects the valuation and key metrics of the combined firm and is closely examined in relation to expected synergy.

2.3.1. *Ownership*

Choice of payment also affects the **ownership structure** of a firm. A cash payment involves no share issuance and leaves the acquirer's ownership structure unchanged. In a stock payment, however, shareholders of the target firm receive stock from the acquirer in exchange for their holdings, and thus become new shareholders in the acquirer. The resulting ownership structure depends on the relative value of each of the combined firms and the level of premium paid for the target firm. In the above example, the shareholders of the target firm receive 100 million shares in a stock-for-stock acquisition. This means that they obtain 50 percent of the voting rights of the combined firm in total, and any additional premium gives these shareholders more votes.

The acquisition of a relatively large firm in a stock-for-stock deal often results in an ownership structure wherein the acquirer is in large part owned by the former shareholders of the target firm because of the relatively large number of shares issued for payment. But if the target firm has unused debt capacity, utilization of that capacity will allow an acquisition to be made without any dilution of the acquirer's ownership. This is typical of leveraged buyouts (LBOs), in which a highly-leveraged special purpose vehicle purchases all of the shares of a target firm and merge with it immediately after the transaction. Through the merger, the debt owed by the vehicle becomes that of the target firm. In this form of transaction, the acquirer, which lacks debt capacity per se, pays in cash by issuing debt backed by the assets of the firm to be acquired, and thereby maintains voting control over the firm after the transaction.

3. Legal Frameworks

While mergers and acquisitions are an economic activity, they are based on legal foundations given that corporations are legal entities created by corporate law. Moreover, they require contractual agreements between sellers and buyers, and are subject to financial regulations when the target is a publicly listed firm. We cover such legal aspects in this section, by looking first at the legal forms of mergers and acquisitions, and then at the major characteristics of contractual arrangements, mainly in relation to the valuation of target firms. Finally, we discuss how takeover bid (TOB) rules and appraisal rights, whose main objective is the protection of minority shareholders, are positioned in the context of financial regulations.

3.1. Legal structures

3.1.1. Merger

In a **merger**, one firm, the *surviving* corporation, takes over the businesses of another firm, the *merged* corporation, which ceases to exist. The shareholders of the merged corporation typically receive stock in the surviving corporation, but payment can be in cash or a combination of the two. If stock is used, the shareholders are able to defer paying tax until they sell the shares received.

When payment is made using stock from the parent firm of the acquirer, rather than stock from the acquirer itself, the transaction is called a **triangle merger**. Such a merger involves an acquirer, its parent, and a target (Figure 5.2). In this case, the shareholders of the target firm become shareholders of the parent firm, not of the acquirer itself. This form is used when a parent wants to retain full ownership of a subsidiary that acquires a target firm. The ownership structure of the parent firm changes to reflect the addition of the former shareholders of the target firm.

After the acquisition, the subsidiary acquirer and the target firm often merge to become a wholly owned subsidiary of the parent firm. If the

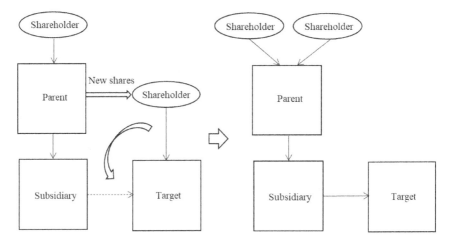

Figure 5.2   Triangle merger.

subsidiary acquirer is the surviving corporation, the transaction is called a *forward* triangle merger. If the target firm is the surviving corporation, it is a *reverse* triangle merger. The latter form is used when the business of the target firm requires licenses that cannot be succeeded to if it merges into another corporation.

3.1.2. Share purchase

A **share purchase** is the most simple, direct form of acquisition in that ownership of the stock of the target firm is transferred to the acquirer, with both the acquirer and the target firm continuing to exist as separate corporations. As with mergers, payment may be made in cash, stock, or a combination of the two, and the tax effect is the same as well. If the acquirer merges with the target firm after the purchase, the result is exactly the same as with a direct merger. Unlike a merger, however, a share purchase may be completed without obtaining approval at the shareholders' meeting of the target firm, provided that each shareholder agrees with the acquirer to sell its holdings.

An acquirer can purchase shares in the public markets if the target firm is listed, but it can also negotiate private trades with blockholders such as institutional investors and founding families. The acquirer will sometimes proceed to a TOB (tender offer) in the public markets after privately acquiring some shares as a *toehold*.

As it does for the parent firm in a triangle merger, a share purchase insulates the acquirer from the liabilities of the target firm in that the latter is a separate corporation and the acquirer is protected by limited liability as its shareholder. A direct merger does not have this insulating effect, because all of target's assets and liabilities are taken over by the surviving corporation.

3.1.3. Asset purchase

Unlike a merger or a share purchase, an **asset purchase** is one in which the acquirer assumes only the assets of the target firm but not its liabilities, although it may agree to undertake the latter as well. Payment is typically made in cash. The seller may be liquidated after the sale, depending on the relative size of the sold assets.

In terms of liabilities, an asset purchase has an advantage in that the acquirer is insulated from any potential liabilities of the target firm as a whole, as the transaction is limited to specified assets. In return for the benefit to the acquirer in being able to purchase assets selectively, the form requires that the transferred assets be specified as such, and this can make a long list. It is also necessary to identify and transfer individual contracts related to the purchased assets, including employment contracts related to any transferred business.

3.1.4. Spin-off

A **spin-off** is a form of divestiture by which a parent firm distributes to its shareholders all of its subsidiary's stock to be divested (Figure 5.3). A firm often carves out one of its businesses into a wholly owned subsidiary as preparation for a subsequent spin-off. A firm's distribution of a subsidiary's stock is economically similar to paying cash dividends to its shareholders, although the latter is a more common form of payout. The shareholders then have direct ownership of the shares of the former parent and its subsidiary.

After a spin-off, the two firms are operated independently as separate entities, each focusing on its own business. While the two firms have the same set of shareholders at the time of such a transaction, this may change from the moment of the transaction if their shares are traded in the public markets.

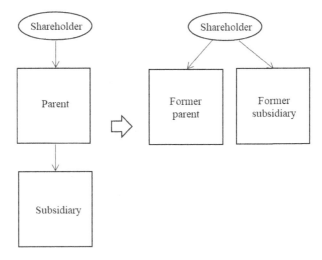

Figure 5.3   Spin-off.

3.1.5. *Split-off*

A **split-off** is similar to a spin-off, but different in that shareholders receive the subsidiary's stock only *in exchange for* its parent's stock. Unlike a spin-off, this exchange decreases the number of shares outstanding for the parent firm. A split-off thus has the economic effect of simultaneously executing the sale of a business and the repurchase of shares by the amount of the proceeds.

Since only those shareholders that surrender the parent's stock receive stock in the subsidiary, the split-off subsidiary essentially takes over part of the shareholder base of its former parent (Figure 5.4). A self-selection of sorts occurs through such an exchange, wherein shareholders that are more willing to invest in the subsidiary than in the parent firm leave the shareholder base of the parent, while shareholders with the opposite preference remain with the parent.

The decrease in the number of shares outstanding through the exchange offsets the fall in the value per share of the parent firm which would otherwise result from the divestiture. More specifically, while a divestiture decreases the consolidated earnings, and thereby the value, of the divesting firm, a split-off offsets the downward effect by requiring that

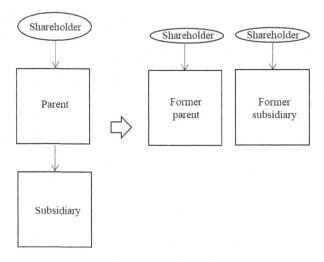

Figure 5.4 Split-off.

shareholders surrender their holdings at an equal value to that of the divested stock. The reduced number of shares outstanding brought about by the surrendering offsets the decrease in earnings, preserving the value per share to the extent that the exchange ratio fairly reflects the relative earning power of the divesting parent and the divested subsidiary. The effect is somewhat mitigated, however, if the parent decides to offer a premium to promote the exchange by adjusting the exchange ratio in favor of the subsidiary stock.

Both spin-offs and split-offs can be executed without incurring tax liabilities at the time of transaction, as these can be deferred until the shares received by shareholders are actually sold. This tax-free treatment gives these forms an economic advantage compared to a divestiture in exchange for cash. An obvious drawback, though, is that a divesting parent cannot receive cash through these transactions even if it should need it.

3.1.6. Carveout

A **carveout** is the partial sale of a subsidiary's shares by its parent, typically in exchange for cash. The process of creating a wholly owned subsidiary from inside a firm, often for the purpose of a future sale, is also called a carveout. In contrast to an outright sale, a partial sale is made for various reasons: It may be to free up capital to invest in other businesses while maintaining a level of influence necessary for the parent firm's business operations; to create a business partnership with a specific buyer with which to form a joint venture; or to provide a transition period for a complete change in ownership, after which the parent firm will sell off the remaining holdings. When cash is used to pay for a partial sale, the parent firm immediately becomes liable to a capital gains tax.

A parent company may also choose to publicly list part of its shareholdings for a carveout instead of negotiating with a specific acquirer in private. However, a listing of this sort creates a conflict of interest between the controlling parent firm and other **minority shareholders**. Some Japanese firms with a number of listed subsidiaries, such as Hitachi and Sony, have addressed this since the late 2010s by unwinding such dual listings, either by making them wholly-owned subsidiaries or by selling them off to third parties.

3.2. Contractual arrangements

Agreements on mergers and acquisitions are set down in a contract, one of the key items of which is the price of the target firm. Negotiations over the target's price, or valuation, are accompanied by a high level of uncertainty owing to the **asymmetric information** held by buyers and sellers. Even when both parties desire to reach an agreement, this asymmetry can stand in the way. To address this issue, some **contractual arrangements** serve to facilitate an agreement by mitigating the impact of asymmetric information.

For instance, some contractual clauses make the price conditional on future events, as we shall see below. In such cases, the price stated in the contract is not a numerical one, but something defined by language, to be finalized in time after the asymmetry is resolved, even after closing. Other clauses enable the parties to withdraw from the contract before closing should certain events or actions, defined in the contract, occur; the agreed price is conditional on their nonoccurrence. In this section, we look at clauses of representations and warranties, earnout, material adverse change (MAC), and breakup fees as examples of such facilitating functions of contracts.

3.2.1. Representations and warranties

Since the valuation of a target firm is based on its current status and future prospects, its private information is usually disclosed through the **due diligence** process, wherein potential acquirers are given access to a physical or virtual data room for review. However, there are two layers of asymmetric information in the process.

One layer derives from limitations on the time and scope of the information disclosed by the target firm. Typically, the time allowed for due diligence is specified in the schedule for the transaction, and the target firm may exclude key items from disclosures made within that timeframe. Information that affects future competition, for example, such as customer lists and pricing policies, may be limited at will or under competition laws, because candidate acquirers in the same industry may change their marketing or pricing behavior after reviewing it, even if the transaction is aborted. For this reason, such information is disclosed, if ever, only to people not directly in charge of sales and marketing at a potential acquirer, often after being statistically processed.

The other layer of asymmetric information derives from the complexity of an organization. In practice, even insiders find it hard to comprehend full, accurate, and timely information on an organization, given that target firms usually comprise multiple business divisions where information is handled on a need-to-know basis. This gives rise to the risk of negative information being revealed post-deal, even if the managers of the target firm have acted in good faith during the due diligence process.

Such limits and uncertainties, which are inherent in organizational information, make less-informed acquirers unwilling to participate in a transaction without proper protection. To solve this issue of asymmetric information, contractual agreements typically include **representations and warranties**, by which the target firm or its shareholders guarantees the accuracy of material information disclosed and the nonexistence of undisclosed negative information. These clauses cover areas such as financial conditions, labor and environmental matters, the legal and contractual status of the business, the condition of physical facilities, and the absence of any material changes after due diligence.

The scope of representations and warranties is often a focus of negotiation, the seller wanting it to be narrow and the buyer wanting the opposite. A qualifier is often negotiated, indicating, for example, whether the items covered in representations and warranties involve *actual* knowledge or *constructive* knowledge. For a target firm, the former means a narrower scope of liability; the latter can include information that the target firm, or its managers, can be expected to have known in their capacity. Despite often intense negotiations, such a clause facilitates an agreement in that it adjusts and mitigates the asymmetric information between the parties by putting the major burden on the more informed party (the seller), to the comfort of the less informed (the buyer). Since even the seller may not be fully confident about its internal information, it may purchase liability insurance when taking on the burden of covering potential loss that could arise should it inadvertently breach the clause.

3.2.2. *Earnout*

Given that valuation depends on the expected performance of the target firm, it can be useful to make the price contingent upon future events, such as the successful development of a medicine by a pharmaceutical firm, or the achievement of an earnings target.[12] Under an **earnout** clause, the buyer and seller agree that the former will make an additional payment if specified business milestones or financial metrics are achieved by the target firm after the transaction. A contingency payment will also facilitate an agreement, particularly in cases where a buyer and seller cannot reach an agreement because of divergent views on the target firm's prospects. By translating uncertainty into a conditional payment, an earnout clause has the effect of mitigating asymmetric information between the parties.

Let us look at an example in Table 5.2. Suppose that a buyer and seller disagree on the prospects of a target firm. The buyer values the firm at $100 million in a good state and $60 million in a bad state. In contrast, the seller values it at $80 million in a good state and $50 million in a bad state.

Table 5.2   Using earnout.

State	Good	Bad	Expected value
Buyer	$100 mil.	$60 mil.	$80 mil.
Seller	$80 mil.	$50 mil.	$65 mil.

---

[12]Choi, A. H. (2016). Addressing informational challenges with earnouts in M&A. In C. A. Hill and S. Davidoff Solomon (eds.), *Research Handbook of Mergers and Acquisitions*. Cheltenham, UK: Edward Elgar, pp. 154–180.

If both parties agreed on the firm's prospects for the future, they will agree on a valuation somewhere between $100 million and $80 million in a good state and between $60 million and $50 million in a bad one. Or, they will agree based on expected value, which would be between $80 million and $65 million assuming they agree on a probability of 50 percent for each state. An agreed price point within each range reflects the bargaining power of both parties as to the distribution of the transaction's benefits.

However, the parties may differ in their subjective assessments of which state will prevail in the future, and in this case there will be no agreement. For instance, if an optimistic seller foresees a good state while a cautious buyer foresees the opposite, the two parties will fail to reach an agreement because the maximum price that the buyer is willing to pay in a bad state, which is $60 million, is lower than the minimum price that the seller is willing to accept in a good state, which is $80 million.

Even in this case, they can still reach agreement by introducing an earnout clause, by which the two parties agree to a price of $60 million, with the additional agreement that the buyer will pay an extra $20 million based on a metric of the target firm, such as its earnings level, that will only be achieved if the target firm is in a good state. The metric needs to be one that can be clearly defined and verified. Under this agreement, when the state of the target firm is actually good, the seller receives a total of $80 million, the minimum price that it is willing to accept in such a state. Similarly, when its state is actually bad, the buyer finalizes the price at $60 million, the maximum price that it is willing to pay in such a state but still above the $50 million which is the minimum price that the seller will accept. In this way, by making the extra payment contingent upon the target firm's state, the buyer and seller are able to reach an agreement desirable to both.

3.2.3. Material adverse change

Where uncertainty is concerned, an extraordinary event can significantly affect a transaction's underlying assumptions. To deal with the uncertainties of unpredictable events, a **MAC** clause is often included so as to give the acquirer leeway to cancel the transaction without liability before the closing. While the cancellation of a transaction that has been agreed upon can have a negative impact on a seller preparing for a closing, the parties will typically agree to this clause in order to protect the acquirer from having to purchase an asset even if its actual value has plummeted.

Such a design is valuable in that it addresses extreme levels of uncertainty and thereby facilitates an agreement. For the seller, however, it also undermines the predictability of the transaction, and for this reason its stipulation is limited. Its scope in practice is so limited that the experience of the COVID-19 pandemic led to parties explicitly *excluding* the effects of the disease from the MACs agreed to in a transaction.[13]

As a corollary, the managers of a target firm generally are obligated to continue running the firm as usual following an agreement. If material changes are made to its business between the agreement and the closing, as they sometimes are, these are subject to approval by the acquirer. A breach of these arrangements may lead to similar consequences to those for a MAC.

3.2.4. Breakup fee

A **breakup fee** is the compensation that a target firm agrees to pay to its would-be acquirer should it decide to cancel a transaction in favor of another acquirer. This can occur because the directors of a target firm, generally in the U.S., owe a **fiduciary duty** to ensure that a sale is in the best interests of its shareholders.[14] Hence the clause is also called a *fiduciary out*. Target firms face uncertainty as to whether the price offered by a prospective acquirer is the best price possible. A fiduciary out mitigates this concern by subjecting the agreed price to a market check and giving other potential candidates a chance to take over the transaction. It thus makes an agreement easier to reach by conditioning it upon confirmation by the target firm that no more attractive acquirer exists.

A contract including this clause often stipulates the fee to be paid by the target firm in the event of its withdrawing from the agreement in favor of another prospective acquirer with a more attractive offer. The fee is typically set at 2–5 percent of the transaction value in the U.S., but around 1 percent in the U.K.[15] In Japan the fee is set at a similar level to the U.S., although clauses like these are used less frequently in Japan.

---

[13]Subramanian, G. and Petrucci, C. (2021). Deals in the time of pandemic. *Columbia Law Review*, 121(5), 1405–1480.

[14]Revlon, Inc. v. MacAndrews & Forbes Holdings, Inc., 506 A.2d 173 (Del. 1986).

[15]Davies, P., Hopt, K., and Ringe, W. G. (2017). Control transactions. In R. Kraakman, J. Armour, P. Davies, L. Enrique, H. Hansmann, G. Hertig, K. Hopt, H. Kanda, H. Pargendler, W. G. Ringe, and E. Rock (eds.), *The Anatomy of Corporate Law: A*

This fee is justified to the extent that it ensures the prospective acquirer's reimbursement for the expenditures it has made in researching the target firm and negotiating the transaction. Otherwise, any new acquirer would enjoy a free ride, taking advantage of efforts that have crystallized in price information on the target firm to offer a price that just exceeds it. However, a fee that is set too high can also hinder a transaction desirable for shareholders by making it costly to switch to another candidate.

There is also a **reverse breakup fee**, which is paid to a target firm by a would-be acquirer when the latter decides to cancel an acquisition agreement. This occurs when the acquirer fails to secure financing to close the deal. Typically, this provision is found in contracts where the acquirer is a private equity fund, which relies on external debt financing for acquisitions.

3.3. TOB rules

When the target of an acquisition is a listed firm, an acquirer will often make a **TOB (takeover bid)**, or a **tender offer** as it is called in the U.S., by which it publicly offers shareholders an equal opportunity to sell their holdings at the same price for a certain period, such as 40–60 days, with disclosure provided for their decision. During this period, the acquirer is prohibited from purchasing the firm's shares in the market. Payment for the shares is made in cash (a *cash offer*) or with stock from the acquirer (an *exchange offer*). A major objective of rules on TOBs is to secure a process that treats shareholders equally when facing a possible change in control.

If an acquirer is to obtain ownership exceeding a certain threshold, the rules require it to follow a formalized TOB process rather than privately negotiate a purchase with shareholders. The threshold triggering this requirement is a purchase of 30 percent or more shares in the U.K. and most EU member states, including Germany;[16] more than 30 percent in

---

Comparative and Functional Approach, 3rd ed. Oxford, UK: Oxford University Press, pp. 205–242.

[16]Rule 9.1, The City Code on Takeovers and Mergers (Takeover Code), 12th ed., The Panel on Takeovers and Mergers; Sections 29-2 and 35, Wertpapiererwerbs- und Übernahmegesetz (Securities Acquisition and Takeover Act).

France;[17] and more than a third in Japan.[18] The idea originated with the U.K. **Takeover Code**, which the EU Takeover Directive took as its model in 2004. The EU member states have discretion in setting their own local laws under the directive, however.[19] The U.S. does not have equivalent rules on triggering a mandatory offer, although acquirers do need to follow a similar set of rules, including disclosure requirements, to make a tender offer in that country.

When a TOB begins, the rules require the board of directors of the target firm to express an opinion on the bid. For instance, if the offer is a hostile one and the board believes that the offer price or premium is too low in light of the intrinsic value of the firm, it may oppose the offer. An acquirer may raise its offer price to gain the support of the board, or it may proceed despite the board's opposition since the ultimate decision lies with the shareholders. If the takeover is a friendly one and the board believes the offer price to be appropriate, it may give the bid its support, often subject to a market check to ascertain that there is no offer of greater benefit to the firm's shareholders. A TOB process typically involves communications and negotiations, in public and private, between the acquirer and the board of the target firm over the board's ultimate stance on the offer. Engaging in this process is one of the fiduciary duties of directors.

U.K. and EU rules oblige an acquirer to offer to purchase the holdings of *all* shareholders when a given threshold is hit, namely 30 percent of shares or more in the U.K. and Germany,[20] and more than 30 percent in France.[21] This means that an acquirer may have to purchase all shares in the potential acquisition even if it wants less than full ownership. In Japan the threshold is higher at two-thirds or more, meaning that the

---

[17]Section 234-2, Règlement Général de L'autorité des Marchés Financiers (General Regulations of the Financial Market Authority).

[18]Section 27-2, Financial Instruments and Exchange Law (FIEL).

[19]Directive 2004/25/EC of the European Parliament and of the Council of 21 April 2004 on takeover bids.

[20]Rule 9.1, The City Code on Takeovers and Mergers (Takeover Code), 12th ed., The Panel on Takeovers and Mergers; Section 32, Wertpapiererwerbs- und Übernahmegesetz (Securities Acquisition and Takeover Act).

[21]Section 231-6, Règlement Général de L'autorité des Marchés Financiers (General Regulations of the Financial Market Authority).

acquirer can limit its offer to a purchase of more than a third but less than two-thirds in a TOB.[22] To different degrees, these rules provide shareholders with the opportunity to sell out their holdings when a **controlling shareholder** emerges, when they would otherwise be left with a minority position. However, by requiring a willingness to make a full acquisition, these thresholds also make the partial acquisition of a firm difficult. Thus they raise the bar for acquisitions overall.

In contrast, U.S. rules protect **minority shareholders** by imposing fiduciary duties on controlling shareholders vis-à-vis minority ones.[23] This is uncommon in the U.K., the EU, and Japan, which provide process-oriented protection. The U.S. rules are viewed as *ex post* rules, by which minority shareholders are given post-transaction protection through court proceedings, while those of Europe and Japan are *ex ante* rules, by which minority shareholders are given pre-transaction protection through a mandatory process under financial regulation.

3.4. Appraisal right

When a merger or acquisition takes place, the target firm may be required to obtain approval at its shareholders' meeting, particularly when the shareholders must surrender their holdings for a merger or other reorganization. The threshold required for such an approval is a majority in some jurisdictions, including the U.S. state of Delaware, but higher in Europe, where it is from two-thirds to 75 percent,[24] and Japan, where it is two-thirds.[25] Even a formally approved deal can have dissenting minority shareholders who desire to hold onto their shares but must give them up in return for a cash or stock payment, according to the terms of the transaction. If a stock-for-stock transaction is approved, even the dissenting shareholders of the target firm must accept the acquirer's shares in exchange for their original holdings.

---

[22] Section 27-13, Financial Instruments and Exchange Law (FIEL).
[23] See footnote 15.
[24] Directorate-General for Competition, The European Commission (2016). Support study for impact assessment concerning the review of Merger Regulation regarding.
[25] Section 309, the Companies Act.

Further, when an acquirer succeeds in obtaining a significant stake in a target firm through a TOB or a block trade with major shareholders, dissenting minority shareholders may be forced out of the target firm even without a vote. This is called a **squeeze-out**, by which a controlling shareholder is allowed to buy out the stock held by minority shareholders without their consent in exchange for payment, typically in cash. In Delaware, the threshold required to enable such a compulsory, short-cut exchange is a majority, though the burden of disclosure and process required of the acquirer is lighter under 90 percent ownership.[26] The practice is possible with 90 percent ownership in most other jurisdictions, including the U.K.,[27] France,[28] and Japan,[29] and with 95 percent ownership in Germany.[30] In this way, an acquirer can achieve full ownership of a target firm even if minority shareholders are opposed.

Because of the compulsory nature of such transactions, corporate law gives minority shareholders an **appraisal right**, by which they make a court claim for payment of the fair value of their original holdings. In the end, this fair value might be the same price as that agreed upon by the acquirer and the target firm's majority shareholders, as some recent U.S. cases show,[31] or even a price that subtracts the value of expected synergy from the agreed price.[32] However, the right to seek fair compensation is essential to protect minority shareholders under a decision rule that is based on a majority or supermajority of shareholders; otherwise, conflicted majority shareholders may be induced to set a price that is less than fair in order to minimize payments to minority shareholders and thereby improve the value of their own holdings. Such institutional protection of fairness in value makes dispersed, minority shareholders willing to participate in, and thereby increases the depth of, the financial markets.

---

[26] Sections 251 and 253, Delaware General Corporation Law.

[27] Section 979, the Companies Act of 2006.

[28] Section L433-4, Code Monétaire et Financier (Monetary and Financial Code).

[29] Section 179, the Companies Act.

[30] Section 327, Aktiengesetz (Stock Corporation Act).

[31] DFC Global Corp. v. Muirfield Value Partners, L.P., 172 A.3d 346 (Del. 2017); Dell, Inc. v. Magnetar Global Event Driven Master Fund Ltd., 177 A.3d 1 (Del. 2017).

[32] Veriton Partners Master Fund Ltd. v. Aruba Networks, Inc. (*Aruba II*), 210 A.3d 128 (Del. 2019).

At the same time, the right to protection is also prone to abuse, as it gives investors opportunities to profit from it, for example by purchasing shares *after* a transaction is announced, and filing a lawsuit claiming damages or compensation as dissenting shareholders. In the U.S., where 96 percent of mergers are challenged in courts, Delaware changed its laws to make it more difficult for plaintiff investors to win legal challenges to mergers and for plaintiffs' counsels to collect fee awards, although the result has been an increase in filings in other states and the federal courts.[33]

4. Anti-takeover Measures

Faced with the threat of a **hostile takeover**, firms may institute **anti-takeover measures**. These include arrangements written into articles of incorporation as well as practical behaviors taken in response to a threat. While such measures may effectively inhibit a sudden, uninformed change in control, where shareholders have not had time to decide whether a proposed hostile acquisition would be desirable, they can also result in managers entrenching themselves for their private benefit. Therefore, shareholders tend to view such defensive measures with a degree of caution. The U.K. restricts firms from adopting anti-takeover defenses during the course of a TOB, or even before one, unless approval has been obtained at a shareholders' meeting. This is called the **non-frustration rule**, and is stipulated in the Takeover Code.[34] Other jurisdictions also require shareholder approval in principle, even though they may allow a target firm to adopt a temporal defensive measure based solely on the approval of its board of directors.

Governments, meanwhile, often screen investments by foreign acquirers in key industries, even when a transaction has been agreed upon at the firm level. Such intervention, while out of a firm's purview, can be seen as a kind of anti-takeover defense set by governments for key industries.

---

[33]Cain, M. D., Fisch, J., Davidoff Solomon, S., and Thomas, R. S. (2018). The shifting tides of merger litigation. *Vanderbilt Law Review*, 71(2), 603–640.

[34]Rule 21.1, The City Code on Takeovers and Mergers (Takeover Code), 12th ed., The Panel on Takeovers and Mergers.

4.1. Anti-takeover defenses by firms

One common provision adopted by firms is the **poison pill**. This is a mechanism under which a firm, with authorization obtained at its shareholders' meeting, dilutes the shareholdings of a hostile acquirer by issuing new shares or rights to its existing shareholders for a nominal price. Martin Lipton, co-founder of the U.S. law firm Wachtell, Lipton, Rosen and Katz, is credited with inventing the structure for a defense by El Paso Electric against General American Oil in 1982. When a threat is imminent, a firm may take this measure with only the approval of its board of directors, but must usually subject it to later approval at a shareholders' meeting. The number of firms using the poison pill defense has decreased in recent years, even in the U.S., where the number of S&P 500 firms adopting it has fallen from 227 in 2005 to only 10 in 2020.[35]

Similarly, a firm may stipulate a **staggered board** in its articles of incorporation, ensuring that the terms of its board members end in different years and that all are not all replaced at one time. Typically, a third of the board's directors will stand for election each year, so that a full replacement takes up to three years. This measure has a defensive effect where directors cannot be dismissed without cause, as may be the case in the U.S. It is not the case in the U.K. and Japan, however, where directors can be replaced without cause following approval obtained at a shareholders' meeting, which a shareholder can call at any time provided they have had a 5-percent stake in the U.K. or a 3-percent stake for the last six months in Japan.[36] When effectively designed, the staggered board arrangement hinders a hostile acquisition by making it costly for a hostile acquirer to raise a target firm's value even when it has succeeded in acquiring a controlling stake. However, as is the case with the poison pill, the percentage of S&P 500 firms taking this measure has declined from 60.0 percent in 2010 to 10.9 percent in 2020.[37]

---

[35]Bab, A. L. and Neenan, S. P. (2011). Poison pill in 2011. *Director Notes*, 3(5), 1–12; Klingsberg, E., Tiger, P., and Bieber, E. (2020). A look at the data behind recent poison pill adoptions. Harvard Law School Forum on Corporate Governance, April 24, 2020.

[36]Sections 168 and 303, the U.K. Companies Act of 2006; Sections 296 and 339, the Japanese Companies Act.

[37]Larcker, D. F. and Tayan, B. (2019). Loosey-goosey governance: Four misunderstood terms in corporate governance. Rock Center for Corporate Governance at Stanford University Closer Look Series, No. CGRP-79, 2019; Tonello, M (2020). Corporate board practices in the Russel 3000 and S&P 500: 2020 edition, the Conference Board.

In contrast, the **golden parachute**, which provides departing managers with a generous severance package upon a change in control, remains widely adopted. This is another form of defense in that it lowers the value of the target firm by the amount paid, thereby entrenching managers. It has a facilitating function at the same time, however, as it reduces the incentive of managers to remain with their firm. It even gives them an incentive to negotiate for a high sale value when the package is contingent on that value. It is therefore a double-edged sword: Golden parachutes have been found to be associated with higher expected acquisition premiums, while firms that use golden parachutes tend to experience negative abnormal stock returns.[38]

In addition to these institutional and contractual measures, a firm may resort to various practical tactics to defend itself. One is partnering with a **white knight**, a firm friendly to the target firm that saves it by acquiring a controlling stake in place of a hostile acquirer. Another is to find a **white squire**, which acquires a stake in the target firm that is less than a controlling one but sufficient to block a hostile takeover. In both cases, the target firm enters into a stronger business relationship with the savior but in a friendly manner.

A firm may also choose to divest its key business, or **crown jewel**, to make itself less attractive to any potential acquirer and particularly a hostile one. The buyer of the crown jewel is sometimes a friendly partner, but may also be a private equity fund which has stand-by capital for a swift acquisition. This tactic is also called the **scorched earth defense**.

4.1.1. *Duties of the board*

Given that anti-takeover defenses can benefit incumbent managers at the expense of shareholders, they may be challenged by shareholders, including potential hostile acquirers. This is an issue that relates to the **fiduciary duties** of the board directors who approve the adoption of such measures. There are key U.S. case laws that provide judicial standards in this regard.

The most notable standard derives from a case involving the oil company Unocal, hence called the **Unocal test**. The Supreme Court of

---

[38]Bebchuk, L., Cohen, A., and Wang, C. C. Y. (2014). Golden parachutes and the wealth of shareholders. *Journal of Corporate Finance*, 25, 140–154.

Delaware required in its adjudication that defensive measures be proportional and reasonable given the nature of their threat to corporate policy, and accepted Unocal's defensive measures as valid under that test.[39] Immediately after the Unocal case, however, the court established the **Revlon duties**, which restricted the discretion of directors over defensive measures in a case involving the cosmetic company Revlon. It decided that the role of a board of directors changes from "defenders of the corporate bastion" to "auctioneers" at the time of the sale or breakup of a firm, and that it has a fiduciary duty to maximize shareholder value.[40] This means that a defensive measure, even one which has passed the Unocal test, will not be permitted if it is detrimental to shareholder value. The Revlon case is often cited in support of arguments for maximizing shareholder value in decisions by boards of directors, even in contexts other than a firm's sale.

The recent decline in anti-takeover measures implies that shareholders lack confidence in their ability to enhance firm value. Since there is no point in a hostile takeover if a firm is being run at its highest possible value, the best anti-takeover measure is financial management that maximizes value. The concept of the **market for corporate control** derives from the view that managers will be replaced by those with better skills and ideas,[41] and it is realized only in a world without frictions that mitigate against change in control. Anti-defensive measures can typify such frictions when abused, and are generally viewed with caution.

4.2. Government intervention

At the government level, a recent trend is for governments to intervene in cross-border acquisitions which they perceive to be a threat to the national interest. Governments in general have promoted **foreign direct investment (FDI)** under the liberalization of capital movement made possible by bilateral and multilateral free trade agreements. But it is notable that these governments leave room for public intervention in cross-border investments out of concern for national security. This perspective is separate to those underpinning governmental competition laws.

---

[39] Unocal Corp. v. Mesa Petroleum Co., 493 A.2d 946 (Del. 1985).
[40] Revlon, Inc. v. MacAndrews & Forbes Holdings, Inc., 506 A.2d 173 (Del. 1986).
[41] Manne, H. G. (1965). Mergers and the market for corporate control. *Journal of Political Economy*, 73(2), 110–120.

As one example, the U.S. government reviews FDIs that might affect national security, and the president has the authority to block them. The review is carried out by the Committee on Foreign Investment in the United States (CFIUS), chaired by the secretary of the Treasury. The committee is authorized under the Exon-Florio amendment to the Defense Production Act of 1950, part of the Omnibus Trade and Competitive Act of 1988.[42] The amendment was prompted by an attempt by Fujitsu, a Japanese electronics firm, to acquire Fairchild Semiconductor International. The committee was given wider authority under the Foreign Investment and National Security Act of 2007[43] and by the Foreign Investment Risk Review Modernization Act (FIRRMA) of 2018.[44] In 2018, 2019, and 2020, 8.7 percent, 4.3 percent, and 3.4 percent, respectively, of transactions were either abandoned or blocked.[45]

The EU, meanwhile, introduced in 2019 an FDI screening regulation which went into effect in the following year.[46] The regulation is intended to coordinate the screening mechanisms of member states, and focuses on threats to the security or public order of EU countries. In the U.K., the government was authorized to issue public intervention notices in matters involving national security and financial stability, as well as media quality, plurality and standards, even before 2021.[47] The country strengthened its regulation that year, however, by introducing a broader review system which enables the government to block investments that have material influence on or cause a risk to national security.[48] The discussion on intervention was prompted by the takeover of Cadbury by Kraft in 2010 and that of Arm by Softbank in 2016.[49]

---

[42] Section 5021, Omnibus Trade and Competitive Act of 1988, Public Law No. 100-418.
[43] Public Law No. 110-49.
[44] Public Law No. 115-232.
[45] Kaniecki, C. D. and Jaywant, S. (2021). CFIUS releases 2020 annual report, Cleary Foreign Investment and International Trade Watch, June 29, 2021.
[46] Regulation (EU) 2019/452 of the European Parliament and of the Council of 19 March 2019 establishing a framework for the screening of foreign direct investments into the Union, OJ L 791, 21.3.2019, pp. 1–14.
[47] Section 42, Enterprise Act of 2002.
[48] Sections 8 and 26–3, National Security and Investment Act of 2021.
[49] Watson, R. O., Humpe, C., and Kon, S. (2020). Understanding the current rules and regulations around takeovers by overseas buyers. *Macfarlanes*, April 21, 2020.

Similarly, Japan obliges foreign investors to notify authorities of investments in key industries such as energy, telecommunications, transport, space development, water, agriculture and forestry, based on which it may issue orders to unwind or block the investments.[50] Japan also places limits on ownership by foreign investors under laws specifically applied to certain industries and firms. For instance, foreign ownership is limited to a third for airlines, freight transporters and its largest telecommunication firm, Nippon Telegraph and Telephone (NTT), and to a fifth for the largest stock exchange, Japan Exchange Group, and major domestic broadcasters.

In addition to government reviews under competition laws, interventions grounded in national interest are becoming important points to consider when structuring and agreeing upon mergers and acquisitions. While beyond the control of the managers of the firms involved, these phenomena make communicating with governments an integral part of the deal process.

5. Post-merger Integration

An M&A transaction places both the acquirer and the target firm at the starting point of a **post-merger integration (PMI)**. Firms are increasingly being managed as groups, linked with each other in a network of people, capital, and information. The skill with which managers integrate firms joined in a merger or other transaction will affect the economics of the entity that results. Through integration, the acquirer hopes to justify its investment by achieving a level of profitability that exceeds the premium it has paid to the former owner. Integration also affects the acquirer's reputation in the market for corporate control, since few potential target firms would be willing to work with an acquirer with a poor track record of PMI. The track record also matters to private equity funds, whose ability to source acquisition transactions in the market hinges on reputations formed post-deal.

5.1. Realizing synergy

Arguably the most important issue affecting PMI is the appointment of managers to key posts, for these are the people who will control the firm's day-to-day management based on a shared understanding of the acquirer's

---

[50] Sections 26, 27 and 29, Foreign Exchange and Foreign Trade Act.

corporate purpose. The core of PMI is realizing the synergy that is planned at the time of the transaction, on the right timeline and with the right people.

Because firm value is the discounted value of future free cash flow, the timing of effecting synergies is important. It makes an obvious difference, for instance, if a firm reaches a milestone in one year rather than the three years' time that was planned. Key results of PMI, such as the opening of new retail stores for a targeted market share or the launching of a new drug in the pharmaceuticals market, are evaluated not only with regard to whether they are achieved, but also how long they take to be achieved in terms of the time value of money. In the same vein, expected synergies such as sales increases and margin improvements are measured using **key performance indicators (KPIs)** with specific timelines. These are tracked post-merger and are often tied to the incentives of appointed managers.

When a private equity or venture capital fund makes an acquisition, it executes a plan to raise the value of the investee firm and exit the investment within a certain number of years. Because the fund is a financial buyer, its plan does not include business integration with its acquisition, but the investee firm is often plugged into the fund's network of industry information and business contacts, including managerial talent. The fund's portfolio companies in different industries or regions may work together to identify business synergies. Given that a fund seeking to exit an investment not only lists its shares to the public but also sells them off to firms seeking an acquisition, it manages its investee firms from the perspective of making them attractive targets for potential acquirers. Consistent with the fact that the success or failure of a fund investment is clearly visible to underlying investors, funds are rigorous about financial return: financial buyers, such as private equity funds, tend to pay lower premiums than publicly traded industrial firms.[51]

5.2. Control and autonomy

To optimize risk management, an acquirer whose due diligence was limited prior to signing will often conduct further due diligence after

---

[51] Bargeron, L. L., Schlingemann, F. P., Stulz, R. M., and Zutter, C. J. (2008). Why do private acquirers pay so little compared to public acquirers? *Journal of Financial Economics*, 89(3), 375–390.

the transaction. This is done particularly when the contract allows the acquirer to claim damages or compensation against the seller should it find, prior to the contract's expiration, facts that are in breach of the representations and warranties made by the target firm. Post-transaction due diligence also allows the buyer to thoroughly examine and review the risks of the purchased firm, in a manner consistent with the policies and processes of its **internal risk control** system.

In acquiring a startup, a key issue is the **autonomy** and incentives given to the managers of the target firm. When a startup is acquired by a larger firm, factors that are critical to retaining key people include preserving its entrepreneurial culture, as opposed to imposing bureaucracy, and providing appropriate incentive packages. Retention matters, given that most of a startup's value lies in the skills and talents residing inside it. Firms will often deploy an acquisition in place of hiring, in a practice sometimes called "acqui-hiring."[52] **Open innovation**, a strategy by which a firm sustains innovation by internalizing external technology seeds through mergers and acquisitions, alliances, or licensing,[53] shows that success in PMI is essential to a firm's growth in a world of changing and competing technologies.

The skills required to accomplish this extend to **organizational design**. Google, one of the most active acquirers in the technology field, in 2015 created a parent firm, Alphabet, and listed its shares in place of Google's. In doing so it enabled an umbrella structure under which its search engine business is owned by the holding company in parallel with other experimental endeavors such as Waymo autonomous vehicles and DeepMind artificial intelligence technologies. The structure not only makes the individual performance of its existing businesses clearly visible to investors along with other corporate endeavors, but has an additional benefit in that Waymo and DeepMind are not owned by Google but operated in parallel to it under the umbrella of the holding company. This intricate balance between control and autonomy indicates Google's overall willingness to pursue experimental efforts outside of its existing business hierarchy.

---

[52]Chatterji, A. and Patro, A. (2014). Dynamic capabilities and managing human capital. *Academy of Management Perspectives*, 28(4), 395–408.

[53]Chesbrough, H. W. (2003). *Open Innovation: The New Imperative for Creating and Profiting from Technology*. Boston, MA: Harvard Business School Press.

5.3. Failures and overconfidence

Despite the efforts made by firms after a merger, some mergers and acquisitions do, unfortunately, fail, with shareholders incurring losses as a result. Indeed, some divestiture transactions are made by acquirers that find their acquisition underperforming in relation to initial prospects. Toshiba's sale in 2018 of Westinghouse, which it had acquired in 2006, is an example of such a divestiture. A merger may result in a separation, like the breakup of DaimlerChrysler in 2007 following a merger eight years earlier. Such failures may derive from the **hubris** of managers, who would believe themselves more skilled at running the target firm than the incumbent managers or at realizing value through the new combination.[54] This hubris, or **overconfidence**, is confirmed by empirical research: It is found that when managers have a high level of overconfidence, they tend to overestimate their ability to generate returns, while undertaking value-destroying mergers, overpaying on premiums, and incurring large losses for shareholders.[55] Indeed, one estimation finds that 70–90 percent of mergers and acquisitions fail;[56] another finds that one-third of all acquisitions end in failure and an additional one-third fail to live up to expectations.[57]

Overconfidence has also been shown to have positive aspects, however, such as promoting productive and innovative activities as well as concern for others.[58] Overconfident CEOs tend to invest more in innovation and obtain more patents and patent citations in innovative industries.[59] The crucial point, then, is to adopt the positive sides of

---

[54]Roll, R. (1986). The hubris hypothesis of corporate takeovers. *Journal of Business*, 59(2), 197–216.

[55]Malmendier, U. and Tate, G. (2008). Who makes acquisitions? CEO overconfidence and the market's reaction. *Journal of Financial Economics*, 89(1), 20–43; Hayward, M. L. A. and Hambrick, D. C. (1997). Explaining the premiums paid for large acquisitions: Evidence of CEO hubris. *Administrative Science Quarterly*, 42(1), 103–127.

[56]Christensen, C. M., Alton, R., Rising, C., and Waldeck, A. (2011). The big idea: The new M&A playbook. *Harvard Business Review*, 89(3), 48–57.

[57]Bazerman, M. H. and Samuelson, W. F. (1983). I won the auction but don't want the prize. *Journal of Conflict Resolution*, 27(4), 618–634.

[58]Taylor, S. E. and Brown, J. D. (1988). Illusion and well-being: A social psychological perspective on mental health. *Psychological Bulletin*, 103(2), 193–210.

[59]Hirshleifer, D., Low, A. and Teoh, S. H. (2012). Are overconfident CEOs better innovators? *Journal of Finance*, 67(4), 1457–1498.

overconfidence while avoiding the negative ones. It is found that strong and independent boards help overconfident CEOs avoid honest mistakes when seeking to acquire other companies,[60] and that introducing a corporate governance mechanism, as exemplified by the U.S. Sarbanes and Oxley Act, tends to mitigate loss of value caused by mergers and acquisitions.[61]

Given these risks and the relatively high probability of failure, it is fundamental that acquirers thoroughly analyze post-merger plans *before* signing a contract. The core of such analysis must be a valuation of the target candidate, including the premium to be paid for it. Transactions are often made in a competitive setting, however, where multiple buyers vie for a target firm that interests them. When this is the case, there will be layers of private negotiations, or an auction requiring competitive bids, before the transaction takes place. And despite the principle of *caveat emptor*, it will likely result in a **winner's curse**.[62] As with the other aspects of business, experience and preparation matter in mergers and acquisitions. It is found that firms with in-house M&A teams perform better than those that rely on outside experts, unless their CEOs are overconfident or have empire-building aspirations.[63] Organizational knowledge accumulated through a series of M&A decisions makes a buyer's managers wiser and more prepared for the analysis, negotiation and PMI needed for a transaction to generate true value.

At the same time, managers must continuously check their firm's business portfolio to see that it is making best use of capital and people, divesting businesses as needed while pursuing new combinations that advance their strategy. Such strategic reviews are increasingly a key part of board decisions, integral to ensuring that a firm's businesses are in the hands of the best owner.

---

[60]Kolasinsiki, A. C. and Li, X. (2013). Can strong boards and trading their own firm's stock help CEOs make better decisions? Evidence from acquisitions by overconfident CEOs. *Journal of Financial and Quantitative Analysis*, 48(4), 1173–1206.

[61]Banerjee, S., Humphery-Jenner, M., and Nanda, V. (2015). Restraining overconfident CEOs through improved governance: Evidence from the Sarbanes-Oxley Act. *Review of Financial Studies*, 28(10), 2812–2858.

[62]Thaler, R. H. (1988). Anomalies: The winner's curse. *Journal of Economic Perspectives*, 2(1), 191–202.

[63]Gokkaya, S., Liu, X., and Stultz, R. M. (2021). Do firms with specialized M&A staff make better acquisitions? NBER Working Paper, No. 28788.

6. Conclusion

Mergers and acquisitions are a critical part of a firm's growth. They involve many legal aspects, such as the choice of structures, tax considerations, contractual negotiations, risk and liability control, and reviews by authorities for compliance with competition and national security laws. Their importance in bringing discontinuous change to a firm's growth trajectory draws attention even to the psychological aspects of the practice, such as overconfidence. Given that firms grow in a path-dependent manner,[64] different firms are likely to possess different strengths and weaknesses. Mergers and acquisitions enable them to combine these qualities to create new trajectories toward growth. The process comes with risks, however, and the financial markets tend to cast a cautious eye on acquirers that claim to create value through these transactions.

For every firm seeking a merger or acquisition, there is always another that has a business to divest. It may be a competitor in the same industry, or a private equity or venture capital fund seeking an exit to an investment. A decision to divest a business tends to be perceived more positively because it typically gains a premium over its market value and brings greater clarity to the business that remains. For a divesting firm and its shareholders, a divestiture means a recovery of investment, often with a capital gain, which enables them to redirect the capital toward new investment opportunities. If they desire, they may also have an opportunity to invest in the acquirer through an exchange of stocks with the acquirer or investment on their own in the financial markets.

Despite their many complexities and caveats, mergers and acquisitions are a dynamic reallocator of resources in the economy, not only in the form of capital but also as skills, knowledge, and ideas that might otherwise be left unexplored. Changes in corporate boundaries allow buyers to find new synergies, and sellers to improve their focus and generate resources for new investments. Mergers and acquisitions offer managers with an effective way to productively deploy capital and realize the best combinations of business, provided they continuously assess their portfolios and positions in the market.

---

[64]David, P. (1985). Clio and the economics of QWERTY. *American Economic Review*, 75(2), 332–337.

Chapter 6

Managing Shareholder and Stakeholder Value

I. Overview

An established principle of financial management is the **maximization of shareholder value**. It is key to supporting proper functioning in the financial markets where corporations raise and return capital for investors. Without a reasonable expectation that their investments will generate returns, investors are better off not investing at all. In financial terms, maximization of shareholder value is one of the basic premises of a corporation. This notion derives from the corporation's status as a legal format that enables managers and entrepreneurs to raise capital from investors protected by limited liability, and to invest the proceeds in creating and growing business. When managers and investors agree with this notion, it means that both sides believe that managers will act in the best interests of shareholders, even in the face of uncertainty as to how far managers will succeed in doing so.

In line with the principle of maximizing shareholder value, managers are incentivized to increase it. Their compensation design is usually tied to metrics related to short-term value creation, such as annual earnings, and those related to long-term value creation, such as **total shareholder return (TSR)** over the long term. Long-term compensation is often realized by stock compensation in forms such as restricted stock and stock options, with a vesting period of some years, as well as performance-based awards.

Recently, however, performance evaluation criteria often include non-financial metrics as well, which measure things like workforce welfare and carbon footprint. In 2021, for instance, 57 percent of the S&P 500 companies in the U.S. included measures for **ESG (environmental, social, and governance)** goals among their incentives.[1] There are also cases of incentive plans that make the vesting of stock compensation contingent upon ESG performance milestones. These designs reflect a growing need for managers to manage both shareholder value and **stakeholder value**, the latter including factors such as employee wellness, gender equality, customer satisfaction, fair trade in sourcing, and community engagement, as well as environmental sustainability in terms of energy efficiency, waste volumes, carbon emissions, and air and water cleanliness. In part, such moves reflect a recognition that government regulations and interventions can be insufficient when policy actions fail to solve **externalities** imposed by business activities.

The growing interest in stakeholder value does not always align with the maximizing of shareholder value, at least in the short run. Indeed, in a widely known article, the Nobel-laureate economist Milton Friedman asserted in 1970 that the responsibility of managers lies only in maximizing shareholder value under applicable constraints of external regulations, and warned managers against diverging from that path.[2] While some stakeholder-oriented activities do match shareholders' — efforts for greater energy efficiency leading to cost savings, for example — others contradict each other: more generous pay and benefits for employees in a given year mean lower profits for shareholders in the same year, creating at least a short-term **tradeoff** between the two. While the two directions may merge at some point, as when greater pay and benefits lead to higher engagement and employee retention and an increase in shareholder value, these relationships are often vague and hard to identify. Therefore, there is more to understand in order to reconcile the two types of value, shareholder and stakeholder, in managing firms.

Stakeholder value can have diverse definitions. Typically, it points to benefits for employees, customers, suppliers, communities, and the natural environment. In some cases, CEOs may plunge into discussions on social issues which have traditionally been dealt with in the political

---

[1] Semler Brossy Consulting Group (2021). 2021 ESG & Incentives Report, June 14, 2021.
[2] Friedman, M. (1970). The social responsibility of business is to increase its profits. *The New York Times Magazine*, September 13, 1970, 122–126.

arena. This is sometimes called CEO activism,[3] and is notably seen among firms in the U.S. Seen categorically, the components of each category of stakeholder change over time — individual employees join and exit firms; customers and suppliers transact with firms at some point and leave them at another; residents move in and out of communities; environmental damage requiring an urgent response shifts from chemical-derived air and water pollution to global warming and climate change caused by greenhouse gas (GHG) emissions.

Given the diversity of interests, we discuss stakeholder value mainly in terms of environmental protection, which, with its global nature reflected in the Paris Agreement drafted in 2015 and ratified in 2016,[4] has a comparatively common ground across countries. The argument can be extended to other areas in view of the potential for conflicts with shareholder value. Environmental protection is also highly relevant in terms of financial management, in that there is a growing recognition that climate change poses a **systemic risk** to the financial system;[5] this indicates that the environmental impact of a firm's activities translates into a financial impact on the firm itself.

2. Framework of Duties

2.1. Duties of directors

When managers consider stakeholder value, the first question is whether it clashes with the maximization of shareholder value. This question arises because diverging from shareholder value may be against the **fiduciary duties** that managers owe to shareholders under corporate law and case law, particularly in jurisdictions like the U.S. with its traditional notion of shareholder primacy. More precisely, these are primarily the duties of

---

[3]Chatterji, A. K. and Toffel, M. W. (2018). The new CEO activists. *Harvard Business Review*, 96(1–2), 78–89.

[4]United Nations Framework Convention on Climate Change (UNFCCC) (2015). The Paris Agreement, December 12, 2015.

[5]Bank for International Settlements (BIS) (2020). Climate-related financial risks: A survey on current initiatives, Basel Committee on Banking Supervision, April 2020; The U.S. Commodity Futures Trading Commission (2020). Managing climate risk in the U.S. financial system, September 9, 2020.

boards of directors, whose members include the CEO and possibly other senior managers.

As discussed in the previous chapter, an important case law adjudicated in the U.S. in 1986, involving the cosmetic firm Revlon, holds that directors have a fiduciary duty to maximize shareholder value in the context of a firm's sale.[6] The duty to maximize shareholder value, or the **Revlon duty**, has been a central tenet of the fiduciary duties of directors when considering possible conflicts between shareholder and stakeholder value.

Relatedly, the U.S. Department of Labor has published a series of interpretive bulletins on fiduciaries under the **Employee Retirement Income Securities Act (ERISA)**. These define the responsibilities of institutional investors entrusted with retirement assets. Illustrating the tradeoff between shareholder and stakeholder value, they have swung like a pendulum, reflecting the difficulty of handling the emerging tradeoff as well as the political climate: In 2016, the DOL clarified that ERISA fiduciaries could not sacrifice investment returns to promote collateral social policy goals, but that they could consider ESG factors in a risk-return framework, as these might have a direct relationship with the economic value of the plan's investment.[7] In 2018, the department acknowledged that there could be instances when ESG factors present material business risks, but required that ERISA fiduciaries put the plan's economic interests first.[8] Further, in 2020 it removed all explicit references to ESG and required fiduciaries to base their decisions solely on pecuniary factors, even amid mounting opposition.[9] However, the department rolled it back in 2021 by explicitly recognizing in its proposal the potential financial impact of climate change and other ESG factors.[10]

---

[6]Revlon, Inc. v. MacAndrews & Forbes Holdings, Inc., 506 A.2d 173 (Del. 1986).

[7]Employee Benefits Security Administration, Department of Labor (2016). Interpretive Bulletin Relating to the Exercise of Shareholder Rights and Written Statements of Investment Policy, Including Proxy Voting Policies or Guidelines, 81 Fed. Reg. 95,879, December 29, 2016.

[8]Canary, J., Director of Regulations and Interpretations, Employee Benefit Security Administration (2018). Field Assistance Bulletin, No. 2018-01, April 23, 2018.

[9]Employee Benefits Security Administration, Department of Labor (2020). Financial Factors in Selecting Plan Investments, 85 Fed. Reg. 72,846, November 13, 2020.

[10]Employee Benefits Security Administration, Department of Labor (2021). Prudence and Loyalty in Selecting Plan Investments and Exercising Shareholder Rights: Proposed Rule, 86 Fed. Reg. 57,272, October 14, 2021.

More fundamentally, in a case from 1919, a U.S. court related the **discretion** granted to firm managers when making decisions to their duty to maximize shareholder value. It established the **business judgment rule** in reasoning that the managers of Ford Motor Company should be given discretion as long as they pursued the maximization of shareholder value, for instance when deciding whether to drastically lower the price of their cars and expand investment, thus making their products more widely affordable, or to sustain the margin on each car by keeping prices relatively high. Under this doctrine, the courts defer to professional managers in their business decisions and refrain from scrutinizing the validity of the decisions with the benefit of hindsight.[11] Here, the maximization of shareholder value is the basis for the discretion granted to managers by the court's ruling.

Without an expectation that their value will be maximized, shareholders will be highly uncertain about the direction of the firms in which they have invested, headed as they are by managers enjoying wide discretion. They will also be unconvinced that their equity investment will ever prove profitable. This uncertainty will harm firms in turn by making it hard for them to raise the capital they need to invest in projects that will actually create value for their shareholders.

The primary emphasis on shareholder value is reinforced by the requirement that elected directors be approved at shareholders' meetings, a process which forms the source of their legitimacy under corporate law. The law provides that the right to elect board members be granted only to shareholders. It is arguable that managers would violate their duties if they decided to raise stakeholder value at the expense of the shareholders that elect them. Also, it could make for a contradiction if directors claimed legitimacy based on elections at shareholders' meetings on the one hand, while pouring corporate resources into stakeholders' coffers at shareholders' expense on the other.

2.2. Observed diversity

This emphasis on shareholder value, however, is not as distinct in other countries as in the U.S. In an interesting survey published in 1995, managers in the U.S., the U.K., Germany, France, and Japan were asked to

---

[11] Dodge v. Ford Motor Co., 170 N.W. 668 (Mich. 1919).

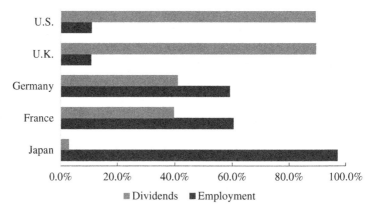

Figure 6.1   Survey of CEOs: Dividends or employment.

Source: Yoshimori, M. (1995). Whose company is it? The concept of the corporation in Japan and the West. *Long Range Planning*, 28(4), 33–44.

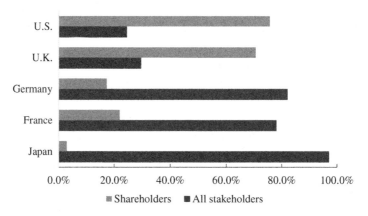

Figure 6.2   Survey of CEOs: Shareholders or stakeholders.

Source: Yoshimori, M. (1995). Whose company is it? The concept of the corporation in Japan and the West. *Long Range Planning*, 28(4), 33–44.

choose between dividends to shareholders and security of employment (Figure 6.1). 89.2 percent of managers in the U.S. and 89.3 percent of those in the U.K. said they would maintain dividends rather than employment, while 97.1 percent of Japanese managers answered that they would prioritize job security over dividends. French and German managers stood in the middle, with 60.4 percent and 59.1 percent of them respectively answering that they would maintain employment rather than dividends.

Similarly, when asked to whom a firm belongs (Figure 6.2), 75.6 percent of U.S. managers and 70.5 percent of those in the U.K. answered that they belong to shareholders, while 97.1 percent, 82.0 percent, and 78.0 percent of Japanese, German, and French managers, respectively, answered that they belong to all stakeholders, including shareholders.[12] Given the increasing globalization of firms over the past few decades, managers today would not give the same answer if asked the same question, but the research points to intrinsic differences in perception regarding who corporations exist for and the purposes they serve. As we shall see in the next chapter, German and French corporate formats give employees, too, a say at the board level, a characteristic unseen in U.S., U.K., and Japanese firms.

While the Japanese corporate format excludes employees from board participation, the emphasis on employment protection is institutionally reflected in labor laws which place stringent conditions on adjusting employment.[13] Also, despite a general belief that independent outside directors serve as defenders of shareholder value and monitor management from that perspective, a survey on the priorities of independent outside directors conducted in 2020 by the Ministry of Economy, Trade and Industry (METI) of Japan reveals that 50.9 percent would act for stakeholders *excluding* shareholders, while 37.6 percent would act for shareholders.[14] Clearly, there is a persistent mentality in Japan that values stakeholders over shareholders.

2.3. Purpose

A similar argument is possible regarding a firm's **purpose**. In 2019, the U.S. Business Roundtable, a group of top managers of major U.S. firms, famously stated that it would place emphasis on stakeholder value as well

---

[12] Yoshimori, M. (1995). Whose company is it? The concept of the corporation in Japan and the West. *Long Range Planning*, 28(4), 33–44.

[13] Section 16, Labor Contract Act ("If a dismissal lacks objectively reasonable grounds and is not considered to be appropriate in general societal terms, it is treated as an abuse of rights and is invalid").

[14] Ministry of Economy, Trade and Industry (METI) of Japan (2020). Practical guidelines for independent directors, July 31, 2020.

as shareholder value as the purpose of a corporation.[15] By putting the purpose up front, the statement shifted discourse on corporate governance from "whose company is it" to "what is a company's purpose," and drew attention to discussions on that question.

"Purpose" is not only a philosophical term, but a legal one in that it is written into articles of incorporation set by firms with the approval of their shareholders. Under the *ultra vires* doctrine, directors are entitled to act only within the limit of the stated purpose. As a matter of legal technique, it is possible, and practical, to describe a firm's purpose as broadly as possible through terms such as "any lawful act"; but, fundamentally, the legal argument over purpose concerns the question of whose interests a firm and its managers serve.

On the one hand, allowing managers to pursue stakeholder value beyond the regulatory requirements and at the expense of shareholders may be a violation of the fiduciary duties of directors to shareholders, because it is not their money, but the shareholders', that would benefit the stakeholders. On the other, such actions may actually help build long-term value for shareholders, in which case they are aligned with the shareholders' interests. In some cases, one could argue that serving the interests of stakeholders leads to greater shareholder value, the only difference being the timeframe.

Here is a case where a conflict of interest between firms and shareholders becomes a question of **time horizon**, even when both accept the emphasis on stakeholder value and its relevance to long-term shareholder value. For shareholders, if long-term value involves too long a timeframe for recovery of their investment, the better course may be to allow the firm to shut down and liquidate rather than pursue it. On the other hand, if **sustainability** is a precondition that must be satisfied regardless of timeframe, it is mandatory for shareholders to embrace it. Otherwise, firms will find their foundations as business entities eroded as the resources contributed by stakeholders are consumed to the extent that employees are exhausted and natural resources extracted. However, it is unclear whether this logic is immune from abuse by managers aiming for greater discretion over their decisions and less intervention by shareholders, as virtually any activity can be connected to the catch-all, powerful objectives of sustainability and long-term value.

---

[15]Business Roundtable (2019). Statement on the purpose of a corporation, August 19, 2019.

By laying out the possible limitations on shareholders as well as stakeholders, the argument over the purpose of a corporation helps to shape **expectations** about the priorities and timeframes of the activities of firms undergoing conflicts and tradeoffs. The contribution of purpose to financial value remains largely ambiguous, but high purpose is associated with the kind of high-clarity workplaces that foster superior performance driven mainly by the middle ranks of the organization.[16]

Shareholders, even when concluding that a firm's purpose is undermining their investment value, would have no problem as long as they are provided with pertinent information, and also with the opportunity, prior to making a decision, to use that information in evaluating their investment. Additionally, shareholders should be able to monitor and verify any measurements that are available on activities concerning stakeholder value, including metrics and narratives. As we shall see, the ability to measure stakeholder value on the basis of purpose is key from this perspective, as it makes the actions of managers more transparent while holding managers accountable to both shareholders and stakeholders.

2.4. Alternative format

One option for alleviating tension between managers and shareholders over stakeholder value is an alternative corporate format, in use in the U.S., which clearly articulates the importance of both stakeholders and shareholders. This is the **public benefit corporation (PBC)**, a for-profit corporation legislated within the framework of corporate law. The Delaware General Corporation Law (DGCL), for instance, added the format in 2015 to its widely-adopted **C-Corporation** format. The law defines public benefit as "a positive effect (or reduction of negative effects) on one or more categories of persons, entities, communities or interests" including "effects of an artistic, charitable, cultural, economic, educational, environmental, literary, medical, religious, scientific or technological nature."[17]

PBCs straddle a line between for-profit and non-profit organizations, as they are expected to generate profits while promoting stakeholder value

---

[16]Gartenberg, C., Prat, A., and Serafeim, G. (2019). Corporate purpose and financial performance. *Organization Science*, 30(1), 1–18.

[17]Section 362(b), Subchapter XV, Delaware General Corporation Law.

at the same time. In 2012, Patagonia became the first company in California to register as a benefit corporation, the state's equivalent to a PBC, with a view to preserving the earth's natural environment.[18] A similar format is seen in France as well: In 2020, Danone converted itself into "société à mission," an equivalent format to a PBC that was created by French law in 2019.[19]

Given that the PBC alternative is relatively new, its early uses mainly involve startups.[20] The PBC format is mainly being adopted in consumer-facing industries, possibly with the aim of appealing to their target markets. Firms with this corporate format are found to be successful in raising capital from traditional venture capital providers, with no significant difference from those using the traditional format of a C-Corporation.[21]

Standards for the fiduciary duties of directors are different from those applied to C-Corporations in that directors *must* consider the benefits of other groups as well as those of shareholders. This implies that the C-Corporation format involves the legal premise of a fiduciary duty to maximize shareholder value, at least in the long run. Choosing a PBC not only signals the intentions of a firm's managers, but means, in legal terms, that the directors are not absolutely required to maximize shareholder value, although the relatively short time since legislation provides little clue as to the scope of fiduciary duty in case law. The choice of a PBC does not mean that managers will no longer need to face a tradeoff between contradicting types of value, because that tradeoff will always exist at times of limited corporate resources.

Changing formats is one way to mitigate this conflict because it clearly lays out the assumptions that shareholders need in making their investment decisions. It is not only legal premises and expectations that are in play, but also human psychology: The added format resonates with the general psychological tendency to make different decisions under

---

[18]Patagonia Works (2013). Annual Benefit Corporation Report, Fiscal Year 2013.

[19]Section 169, Loi n° 2019-486 du 22 mai 2019 relative à la croissance et la transformation des enterprises (Business Growth and Transformation Law).

[20]Dorff, M. B., Hicks, J., and Davidoff Solomon, S. (2020). The future or fancy? An empirical study of public benefit corporations. *Harvard Business Law Review*, 11(1), 113–158.

[21]*Ibid.*

different **framings**.[22] A person plays different roles simultaneously in relation to a firm, as a shareholder, a neighborhood resident, an employee, or a customer. If we support a non-profit in its fund-raising for environmental protection, we frame ourselves as donors and have no expectation of profiting financially from its activities. In contrast, if we invest in a for-profit firm, we frame ourselves as its literal investors and fully expect it to make money for us; we may even make light of any environmental damage it causes along the way as long as it complies with regulations. This seemingly schizophrenic contradiction in response arises because we face differences in framing when making decisions, and adapt our decisions to those differences. The psychological as well as the legal role of the PBC format lies in its affecting this framing upstream, by explicitly putting stakeholder value up front at the level of corporate architecture rather than causing conflicts with the notion of shareholder primacy.

Another, related private initiative is the certified **B Corporation**, which derives from a certification program created by B-Lab, a non-profit organization in the U.S. This certification is not exclusive to PBCs, but applicable to all legal corporate formats. Therefore, the certification does not, by itself, discharge directors from their legal fiduciary duty vis-à-vis shareholders. It may, however, have the effect of aligning the expectations of shareholders with those of managers, in that managers will inform shareholders of their deference to stakeholders in advance. It may have the further effect of signaling, as is generally the case with certifications, that a firm's statements regarding stakeholders are credible in the light of standards set by a third party.

In terms of the expectations formed by shareholders making investment decisions, the use of such alternative formats has the effect of presenting a firm's goals more clearly beforehand. Even if those goals do not exclusively affect shareholder value, shareholders benefit from such clarity in that it gives them more balanced information on which to base their eventual decisions. A lack of clarity in managerial decisions, by contrast, leads to poorer functioning of the financial markets in the first place, as investors will lack the basis on which to form expectations in evaluating and monitoring their investments. And this connects to the importance of disclosure and measurement, which we discuss in the following.

---

[22]Kahneman, D. and Tversky, A. (1983). Choices, values, and frames. *American Psychologist*, 39(4), 341–350.

3. Disclosure and Measurement

3.1. Uncertainty and discretion

In analyzing the management of the two kinds of value, it is necessary to make a distinction between uncertainty and discretion in managerial decisions. Taking environmental protection as an example, a firm may see tighter environmental regulations unexpectedly after an investment by shareholders, and thereby increase the cost of its operations. This is how investment can be affected by **uncertainty** regarding environmental regulations. Because this uncertainty is ever-present, investors assess regulatory risks when making investment decisions and take their impact into account when evaluating their investments. A key assumption here is the belief by investors that managers will always act to maximize shareholder value within the limits of external, regulatory constraints, and that firms will spend only to meet minimum requirements. As long as this assumption holds, investors can reasonably analyze such external factors as risks and make informed decisions. Managers and shareholders thus have a shared perception of an objective function of a corporation, which is that managers will maximize shareholder value subject to external constraints.

Under a common objective of shareholder value maximization, shareholders may even benefit from managerial **discretion**, as managers have various ways to adapt to regulatory changes and thereby maximize shareholder value. For instance, by proactively investing in measures to protect the natural environment beyond the requirements of regulations, managers may ultimately reduce their firms' environmental costs in the future, as preventative investments can be made at a lower cost today. The net present value of doing so may be positive, which is another benefit for shareholders. In this case, acting from a long-term perspective will have a positive impact on shareholder value today. On a different tack, managers may lobby policymakers to relax regulations if they find that the benefits of doing so will exceed its costs. Oil and gas firms may do this when seeking less stringent emission standards for their fossil-fuel products or longer grace periods before the introduction of such standards. While there are many possible ways of dealing with regulations, shareholders have no problem giving managers discretion over the issue because this is a case where managerial actions and shareholder interests are perfectly aligned.

Discretion may harm shareholders, however, when managers' motives are not aligned with theirs. At the extreme end, shareholders will be unsure whether managers will ever maximize their value, even aside from the extent imposed by regulations. For example, if managers choose to spend aggressively to reduce a firm's air and water pollution beyond regulatory requirements, shareholders will not know how far these managers will go and what they, the shareholders, will receive in return. Here, shareholders cannot take for granted the assumption of shareholder value maximization in managerial objectives, even in the long run. In this scenario, investors face a dual uncertainty regarding regulations and managerial policy.

Stakeholder value may indeed be a growing factor in corporate management, but there is still reason to be wary of increased managerial discretion presented as stakeholder value. This is because shareholders find it hard to know if managers are ever really acting to serve their value, or merely consuming their resources for other causes while actually achieving little. This causes a further problem when it is unclear how managers are prioritizing and pursuing their various goals so that shareholders and stakeholders can assess the managers' plans *ex ante* and verify their performance *ex post*.[23]

Even if managers do act in good faith to maximize multiple sets of value simultaneously, the limited scope of human attention means that people who are presented with multiple goals can focus on only just a few.[24] Making the attempt may ultimately undermine stakeholder value by impairing both focus and consistency, with the perverse result of achieving little on any front.[25]

In this regard, the transparency and predictability of managers in forming investors' expectations are key. As long as the objective function is clear — even if multivariable, such as creating shareholder value while conserving the natural environment — investors evaluating their

---

[23] Jensen, M. C. (2002). Value maximization, stakeholder theory, and the corporate objective function. *Business Ethics Quarterly*, 12(2), 235–256.

[24] Ordóñez, L. D., Schweitzer, M. E., Galinsky, A. D., and Bazerman, M. H. (2009). Goals gone wild: The systematic side effects of overprescribing goal setting. *Academy of Management Perspectives*, 23(1), 6–16.

[25] Bebchuk, L. A. and Tallarita, R. (2020). The illusory promise of stakeholder governance. *Cornell Law Review*, 106(1), 91–178.

investments can reasonably consider uncertainties that are out of managers' control.

3.2. Disclosure

A major avenue to addressing the problem of discretion in terms of stakeholder value is the introduction of **disclosure** requirements for firms in the fields of such value. For instance, BlackRock, the largest institutional investor in the world, announced in 2020 that it would place sustainability at the center of its investment approach. Investee firms would now be required to make disclosures based on the **Sustainability Accounting Standards Board (SASB)** guidelines[26] and the **Task Force on Climate-Related Financial Disclosures (TCFD)** recommendations,[27] two widely accepted disclosure frameworks.[28] The SASB guidelines provide sector-specific guidance on ESG topics such as GHG emissions and employee health and safety, as well as on data security, while the TCFD recommendations focus on climate-related topics such as energy management and resource efficiency both generally and for specific sectors.

The announcement was based not on philanthropic principles, but on BlackRock's belief that sustainability is indispensable to a firm's long-term profitability. Institutional investors generally have a keen interest in disclosure in the ESG fields because it relates to **systematic risk** affecting their investments. Institutional investors typically have a diversified portfolio and require a premium only for systematic risk that remains after the idiosyncratic risks of individual firms are diversified away.[29] They therefore have a significant interest in the systematic risk remaining in their diversified portfolio.[30] The U.K. government followed the move by requiring listed firms to make disclosures based on the TCFD framework,

---

[26]Sustainability Accounting Standards Board (SASB) (2017). SASB conceptual framework, February 2017.

[27]Task Force on Climate-Related Financial Disclosures (TCFD) (2017). Final report: Recommendations of the task force on climate-related financial disclosures, June 2017.

[28]Fink, L. (2020). A fundamental reshaping of finance, January 2020.

[29]Sharpe, W. F. (1964). Capital asset prices: A theory of market equilibrium under conditions of risk. *Journal of Finance*, 19(3), 425–442.

[30]Coffee, J. C. (2020). The future of disclosure: ESG, common ownership, and systematic risk. *Columbia Business Law Review*, 2021(2), 602–650.

starting in 2022.[31] The EU also published a proposal to tighten disclosure requirements through the **Corporate Sustainability Reporting Directive (CSRD)**, starting in 2023.[32] The U.S. SEC launched new disclosure requirements in 2022 as well.[33]

Disclosure functions on various fronts. By making managers' activities more transparent, it reduces their discretion in achieving stakeholder value, particularly when objectives and goals are diverse. Regular, consistent disclosure makes it possible for shareholders and stakeholders to compare a firm with its peers and with its own past records, and to evaluate achievements against goals and expectations.

Disclosure further exposes managers to peer pressure in regard to stakeholder value, just as financial disclosure does in regard to shareholder value. Well-established financial measurements are used for comparative evaluations among peers, but it is practically impossible to establish absolute standards as to what constitutes a desirable financial performance. This is because any desirable level is set against the opportunity cost of capital, which, essentially, is set in relative terms by peers. Similarly, an accumulation of non-financial disclosure practices shapes the market norm of what makes for distinguished, acceptable, or laggard corporate practices in terms of stakeholder value. This may reinforce peer pressure to promote stakeholder value, creating a social norm through an aggregation of practices. Importantly, corporate sustainability practices have been shown to converge within a given industry as they become common practice over time.[34] Therefore, the development of disclosure frameworks is a central requirement for understanding the impacts and importance of the various factors that constitute stakeholder value, and for introducing discipline to control manager discretion in this area.

---

[31] UK Department for Business, Energy & Industrial Strategy (2021). Consultation on requiring mandatory climate-related financial disclosure by publicly quoted companies, large private companies and Limited Liability Partnerships (LLPs), March 2021.

[32] European Commission (2021). Proposal for a Directive of the European Parliament and of the Council amending Directive 2013/34/EU, Directive 2006/43/EC and Regulation (EU) No 537/2014, as regards corporate sustainability reporting, April 21, 2021.

[33] The U.S. Securities and Exchange Commission (2022). The enhancement and standardization of climate-related disclosures for investors, Proposed rule, Release Nos. 33-11042; 34-94478; File No. S7-10-22.

[34] Ioannou, I. and Serafeim, G. (2019). Corporate sustainability: A strategy? Harvard Business School Accounting & Management Unit Working Paper No. 19-065.

3.3. Measurement

While progress in building disclosure frameworks helps in shaping norms in the market, a key to this end is reliable **measurements** that are relevant and meaningful for comparisons. Frameworks for stakeholder value have not converged to the same degree as for financial measurements, which have largely merged into the **U.S. Generally Accepted Accounting Principles (GAAP)** and the **International Financial Reporting Standards (IFRS)**. These principles have evolved over the years from their origins as simple double bookkeeping practices invented in Northern Italy somewhere around the 13th century.[35] The objective for reporting frameworks such as the SASB guidelines and TCFD recommendations is to provide established, consistent measurements for corporate activities relating to stakeholder value.

ESG ratings and **indices** are also used to rate and screen firms on activities that contribute to stakeholder value. While efforts to coordinate these measurements are underway, it is fair to say that no mainstream, de facto standard has been achieved as yet, and that the various frameworks still operate with different objectives and viewpoints. This is another indication that stakeholder value can be diverse and variously defined given its fledgling status. The ESG stock indices now being marketed differ in their definitions and measurement methodologies, as well as in the weights given to the various evaluation factors. Their correlation with each other is low, and some show contradicting data even for objective facts.[36] Ratings may even be changed retrospectively, which also undermines their reliability.[37] This contrasts with **credit ratings**, for instance, whose competing providers, such as Standard and Poor's and Moody's, issue differing results but are highly correlative and have established methodologies.

With each of the diverse frameworks competing to be the de facto standard, making comparisons across firms or countries becomes difficult.

---

[35]Lee, G. A. (1977). The coming of age of double entry: The Giovanni Farolfi ledger of 1299–1300. *Accounting Historians Journal*, 4(2), 79–95.

[36]Berg, F., Kolbel, J. F., and Rigobon, R. (2020). Aggregate confusion: The divergence of ESG ratings. MIT Sloan School Working Paper 5822-19.

[37]Berg, F., Fabisik, K., and Sautner, Z. (2021). Is history repeating itself? The (un)predictable past of ESG ratings. European Corporate Governance Institute Finance Working Paper 708/2020.

But a clue to promoting convergence or harmonization is to see relevance to, and impact on, financial measurements as an anchor, the latter being a widely shared and understood result of a long series of developments. Indeed, the wide acceptance of BlackRock's initiative requiring investee firms' reports to be based on the SASB guidelines and TCFD recommendations is not only due to the firm's influence as the world's largest institutional investor, but also because the requirement ties the disclosures to investees' long-term financial value as a systematic risk. In light of the need for coherency in the reporting of financial and sustainability performance, the initiative taken by the IFRS Foundation in 2021 to set and coordinate reporting standards for sustainability performance by establishing the **International Sustainability Standards Board (ISSB)** is a move in a promising direction,[38] not only because of the foundation's experience in setting standards, but also because of its basis in financial reporting practice.[39] The initiative also promotes harmonization through consolidation with the Value Reporting Foundation (VRF), the governing body of the SASB guidelines.[40]

The **Impact-Weighted Accounts Initiative (IWAI)**, led by George Serafeim, is an important scheme that bears upon the relevance of non-financial metrics to financial ones.[41] Through the lens of the IWAI, the performance of firms looks very different. For instance, the environmental damage caused by GHG emissions, sulfur oxide discharge, and water withdrawal from operations by Exxon Mobil is calculated as $38 billion, or 13.6 percent of revenue, compared to $22 billion, or 6.7 percent of revenue, for Shell, and $13 billion, or 5.8 percent of

---

[38] IFRS Foundation (2021a). Proposed amendments to the IFRS Foundation Constitution to accommodate an International Sustainability Standards Board to set IFRS Sustainability Standards, April 2021.

[39] Barker, R., Eccles, R. G., and Serafeim, G. (2020). The future of ESG is...Accounting? *Harvard Business Review*, December 3, 2020.

[40] IFRS Foundation (2021b). IFRS Foundation announces International Sustainability Standards Board, consolidation with CDSB and VRF, and publication of prototype disclosure requirements, November 3, 2021.

[41] Serafeim, G., Zochowski, T. R., and Downing, J. (2019). Impact-weighted financial accounts: The missing piece for an impact economy. White Paper, Harvard Business School, September 2019; Serafeim, G, Park, D. G, Freiberg, D., and Zochowski, T. R. (2020). Corporate environmental impact: Measurement, data and information. White Paper, Harvard Business School, March 2020.

revenue, for BP. For every $100 sales in 2018, Exxon Mobil's emissions of GHGs caused $13.6 in environmental damage, followed by Shell's at $6.7 and BP's at $5.8.[42]

While an emphasis on relevance to financial measurements is a practical entry point for promoting the convergence or at least a better understanding of their mutual relationships, this does not imply a need to convert every measurement into financial or even numerical metrics. That would be an impractical endeavor, considering that measurements related to stakeholder value include a narrative form that financial frameworks almost always fail to capture. Furthermore, people have a tendency to see things based on their own frame of reference, and will take a measurement they are already familiar with and apply it to unknowns.[43] If all one has is a hammer, everything looks like a nail.[44] The result could be a refusal to adopt measurements that cannot immediately be translated into financial value, and this would hinder the development of disclosure and measurement practices and undermine the protection of stakeholder value. An attempt to translate everything into financial metrics could even precipitate the deployment of unreliable conversion methodologies and further undermine the reliability of disclosures. Given the non-financial, and diverse, aspects of stakeholder value, it is more fundamental to select or develop measurements that are appropriate for the purposes and goals of such value.

At the same time, it is unproductive to broaden the scope of stakeholder value measurements without limit. In the ocean of measurements, **materiality** is the key for specific firms and industries. In terms of stock return, it has been shown that firms with good sustainability ratings on material sustainability issues outperform those which rate poorly; but firms with good ratings on immaterial sustainability issues do not significantly outperform firms with poor ratings.[45]

---

[42] Cohen, R. (2021). *Impact: Reshaping Capitalism to Drive Real Change*. New York, NY: Morgan James.

[43] Pronin, E. (2007). Perception and misperception of bias in human judgment. *Trends in Cognitive Science*, 11(1), 37–43.

[44] Maslow, A. H. (1966). *The Psychology of Science: A Reconnaissance*. New York, NY: HarperCollins.

[45] Khan, M., Serafeim, G., and Yoon, A. (2016). Corporate sustainability: First evidence on materiality. *The Accounting Review*, 91(6), 1697–1724.

4. Shareholders and Changing Paradigms

4.1. *Nature of shareholders*

The measurement requirement also relates to the nature of shareholders. Shareholders run the gamut from high-frequency traders to pension funds, each with their individual preferences and horizons. Pension funds invest for the long term, as they need to manage their assets in ways that will match the cash flow needs of their contributors after retirement. These are typically weighted towards passive investments. BlackRock, which is also the world's largest index investor, has little discretion over the selection of its investees, and passively invests in firms in accordance to market indices such as the S&P 500.

Given the potential long-term impacts of ESG issues on their assets, it is not a coincidence that pension funds and index investors are the most vocal in demanding that firms address such issues. In addition to BlackRock's requirement for expanded disclosure, major pension funds have issued a joint statement demanding that firms work towards long-term, sustainable growth and provide complete, consistent ESG information.[46] Their influences seem real, as increases in ownership by the three largest asset managers — BlackRock, Vanguard, and State Street Global Advisors — are found to be associated with decreases in carbon emissions. This is likely because these firms engage with investees with the highest carbon emissions, and demand that they deal with the associated environmental impacts and risks.[47]

Where index investments are concerned, an institutional investor's choice of ESG indices can affect the behavior of firms. In 2016, for instance, Japan's Government Pension Investment Fund (GPIF)

---

[46]California State Teachers' Retirement System (CalSTRS), Government Pension Investment Fund (GPIF), and USS Investment (2020). Joint statement on the importance of long-term, sustainable growth, March 5, 2020; Alberta Investment Management Corporation, British Columbia Investment Management Corporation, Caisse de dépôt et placement du Québec, Canada Pension Plan Investment Board, Healthcare of Ontario Pension Plan, Ontario Municipal Employees Retirement System, Ontario Teachers' Pension Plan, and Public Sector Pension Investment Board (2020). Companies and investors must put sustainability and inclusive growth at the centre of economic recovery, November 25, 2020.

[47]Azar, J., Duro, M., Kadach, I., and Ormazabal, G. (2021). The big three and corporate carbon emissions around the world. *Journal of Financial Economics*, 142(2), 674–696.

introduced an investment program based on ESG indices, including those provided by MSCI, as part of its passive investment schemes. Since it has the largest public pension assets in the world at $1.6 trillion, inclusion in these indices matters for firms, and the program gives them incentives to raise their own ESG standards to the level required for inclusion.[48]

As seen in the ERISA requirements, an emphasis on ESG issues does not imply any compromise on financial returns. Investors show no willingness to accept suboptimal performance as a tradeoff for socially responsible activities.[49] While the relationship between ESG measurements and long-term value is empirically ambiguous,[50] a meta-analysis shows that about 90 percent of empirical research has found at least a non-negative relationship between ESG criteria and financial performance.[51] As investors pay increasing attention to this relationship, some recent research is finding a positive correlation between ESG issues and financial value. Employee satisfaction, for example, is found to have a positive effect on stock performance.[52] Also, ESG investments are shown to have generated resiliently higher returns during the financial crises.[53] The degree of this impact may also relate to national institutional arrangements: Investors require a lower cost of capital for firms with good ESG

---

[48]Government Pension Investment Fund (2021). ESG Report, August 20, 2021.

[49]Renneboog, L., Horst, J. T., and Zhang, C. (2008). Socially responsible investments: Institutional aspects, performance, and investor behavior. *Journal of Banking and Finance*, 32(9), 1723–1742.

[50]Durand, R., Paugam, L., and Stolowy, H. (2019). Do investors actually value sustainability indices? Replication, development, and new evidence on CSR visibility. *Strategic Management Journal*, 40(9), 1471–1490.

[51]Friede, G., Busch, T., and Bassen, A. (2015). ESG and financial performance: Aggregated evidence from more than 2000 empirical studies. *Journal of Sustainable Finance & Investment*, 5(4), 210–233.

[52]Kempf, A. and Osthoff, P. (2007). The effect of socially responsible investing on portfolio performance. *European Financial Management*, 13(5), 908–922; Edmans, A. (2011). Does the stock market fully value intangibles? Employee satisfaction and equity prices. *Journal of Financial Economics*, 101(3), 621–640.

[53]Lins, K. V., Servaes, H., and Tamayo, A. (2017). Social capital, trust, and firm performance: The value of corporate social responsibility during the financial crisis. *Journal of Finance*, 72(4), 1785–1824.

performance, reflecting lower risk, in countries where investor protection is strong.[54]

For a more granular analysis of such factors and institutional settings, further observation of data is essential, as is the continued development of disclosure and measurement practices for stakeholder value. Measurement, after all, is essential to obtaining anything, since we can only get what we measure.[55] Further developments in practice will not only make managers' actions more transparent and predictable to investors, but will enable investors to understand the materiality of different measurements and prioritize them according to, most notably, the potential financial impact of those factors on their investments.

4.2. Paradigm shift

There may also be a relation, albeit a rather circular one, between the linkage in measurements of stakeholder value to financial value and shifts in investors' subjective value. Financial instruments have no *a priori* value assigned in the market, and the markets value what is already valued. If people see that others perceive a thing as valuable, that thing becomes valuable to them as well. Developments in disclosure and measurement practices give investors the means to measure risks they might have previously underappreciated, and thus to understand and control them. This would shift perceptions in the market, creating financial value for measured stakeholder value. Such circular, spiral changes in the order of value constitute a paradigm shift as a whole,[56] in the sense that changes in the cognition of elements of stakeholder value lead to changes in the perception of value in the financial markets.

Evolving measurements of stakeholder value and the analysis of their impact on shareholder value ultimately involve the bigger question of the purpose of corporations and capitalism, whose standard form has been to focus exclusively on shareholder value. Some labels have been

---

[54]Breuer, W., Müller, T., Rosenbach, D., and Salzman, A. (2018). Corporate social responsibility, investor protection, and cost of equity: A cross-country comparison. *Journal of Banking and Finance*, 96(C), 34–55.

[55]Ariely, D. (2010). You are what you measure. *Harvard Business Review*, June 1, 2010.

[56]Kuhn, T. S. (1962). *The Structure of Scientific Revolutions*. Chicago, IL: University of Chicago Press.

coined for a more integrative view, such as **sustainable capitalism.**[57] Capitalism is a paradigm in that it is a fundamental premise of our thinking and beliefs. An observation of apparent anomalies leads us to discover, and believe in, a new paradigm to serve as the prevailing framework for thinking in the next era; this completes the paradigm shift. At Davos in 2016, a statement predating one by the Business Roundtable in 2019 called for "a new paradigm" requiring managers to make fundamental changes in attitude and attention, and consider stakeholder value as an element of sustainable, long-term shareholder value.[58] This was followed by another statement in 2020 which adopted the hybrid term of **stakeholder capitalism.**[59] In general, people don't notice paradigm shifts when they are actually taking place. But certain harbingers, barely noticed at the beginning, may be foretelling such a shift.

5. Conclusion

Managing shareholder and stakeholder value requires a deep understanding of what the latter means, as its scope and definition can be diverse and carry different value points for different people. Transparency is necessary for managers to pursue their multiple goals for stakeholder value, since these can be in conflict with the shareholder value which is a corporation's fundamental premise. Disclosure and measurement practices are important for this purpose, as they identify and clarify what people are likely to value most.

In terms of financial management, the transparency enabled through such disclosure and measurement practices is beneficial for both shareholders and stakeholders, in that it allows for comparisons between competing firms and between the past and present performance of individual ones. In the absence of a single, holistic framework to serve every interest, a selection of frameworks will continue to coexist. Linkage with

---

[57]Strine, L. (2020). Toward fair and sustainable capitalism. The Roosevelt Institute, August 2020.

[58]Lipton, M. (2016). The new paradigm: A roadmap for an implicit corporate governance partnership between corporations and investors to achieve sustainable long-term investment and growth. *International Business Council of the World Economic Forum*, August 2016.

[59]World Economic Forum (2020). Stakeholder capitalism: A manifesto for a cohesive and sustainable world, January 14, 2020.

financial value provides a perspective from which to evaluate a number of factors comprehensively in terms of material financial risks. With the anchoring provided by financial frameworks, differing measurements of stakeholder value will serve us better, with greater consistency and relevance.

Shareholder and stakeholder value management helps ensure that managers are accountable and predictable as they set and pursue multiple goals. It decreases the risk of managers with considerable discretion achieving little in the end due to a lack of focus and consistency. As managers' responsibilities relate to the legal fiduciary duties of directors, which traditionally require shareholder primacy, alternative legal formats are being investigated in hopes of making legal requirements clearer in regard to stakeholder value as well.

Our world is one of evolving values, and measurement methodologies must adapt to these changes. The methodology of financial accounting has evolved over centuries, mainly driven by interest in pecuniary measurements. As frameworks evolve, we get an indication of what people are interested in and pay attention to. Stakeholder value does not always translate into financial metrics, but these developments, by shedding light on the complexities of firm management and its surroundings, give shareholders a better understanding of risks and returns and enable them to evaluate investments amid evolving values.

Chapter 7

Structuring Corporate Governance

I. Overview

Corporate governance is a system of rules, practices, and processes by which firms are directed and controlled.[1] The modern concept of corporate governance originates in the U.K., where a series of corporate collapses prompted the government to establish a framework to ensure that firms were governed properly. The effort was crystallized in the Cadbury Report, issued in 1992 by a committee headed by Sir Adrian Cadbury.[2] The framework evolved into the U.K. corporate governance code, which documents general rules and recommendations and has been regularly revised to date. An effort at harmonization followed, resulting in the G20/OECD corporate governance code first published in 1999.[3] Bilateral and multilateral free trade agreements may also articulate the establishment of corporate governance practices in each signatory country, as seen in the EU-Japan economic partnership agreement that came into effect in 2019.[4]

---

[1] Committee on the Financial Aspects of Corporate Governance (1992). The Financial Aspects of Corporate Governance.

[2] *Ibid.*

[3] OECD (2015). G20/OECD Principles of Corporate Governance, November 30, 2015.

[4] Agreement between the European Union and Japan for an Economic Partnership, Article 15.2. ("Each Party shall take appropriate measures to develop an effective corporate governance framework within its territory, recognising that those measures will attract and encourage investment by enhancing investor confidence and improving competitiveness,

Such moves reflect a growing global interest in corporate governance frameworks as foundations of business activity.

Often, these codes are structured upon the comply-or-explain rule, by which firms may choose not to comply with a code by disclosing its reasons for not doing so. This non-mandatory nature, the idea for which originates in the Cadbury report, enables rules to be introduced earlier than if they were mandatory, as the latter require a general agreement among constituencies. It also allows for a case-by-case application of the framework, depending on the specific circumstances and properties of individual firms, as well as a flexible updating of the code as it evolves along with changes in the economic and financial environment.

The foundation of a corporation lies in corporate law, which defines and validates its distinct characteristics: these include legal personality, limited liability, transferable shares, centralized management under a board, and shared ownership by contributors of equity capital.[5] Among them, it is increasingly important to design corporate governance architecture so as to mitigate potential conflicts arising from the **separation of ownership and control** and **dispersed share ownership**, both of which are rooted in shared ownership and the transferability of shares.[6]

More broadly, the design of corporate governance relates to the balance between shareholders and stakeholders discussed in the previous chapter, as governance is the most important of the three ESG pillars of criteria for institutional investors.[7] Some countries are giving explicit consideration to employees' interests in board design, and board diversity is gathering increasing attention as well.

---

thus enabling best advantage to be taken of the opportunities granted by its respective market access commitments.")

[5]Armour, J., Hansmann, H., Kraakman, R., and Pargendler, M. (2017). What is corporate law? In R. Kraakman, J. Armour, P. Davies, L. Enriques, H. Hansmann, G. Hertig, H. Kanda, M. Pargendler, W. G. Ringe, and E. Rock (eds.), *The Anatomy of Corporate Law: A Comparative and Functional Approach*, 3rd ed. Oxford, UK: Oxford University Press, pp. 1–28.

[6]Berle, A. A. and Means, G. C. (1932). *The Modern Corporation and Private Property*. New York, NY: Macmillan.

[7]Mishra, S. (2020). Survey analysis: ESG investing pre- and post- pandemic. Institutional Shareholder Services, October 13, 2020.

2. Board of Directors

2.1. Board structure

The structure of the **board of directors** is different across jurisdictions, although the basic idea of a board overseeing management is common. As shown in Figure 7.1, the U.S. and the U.K. have a **one-tier board system**, where members of a board form committees responsible for different board functions. These include a nomination committee, a compensation (remuneration) committee, and an audit committee. Financial expertise is a desirable requirement for members of an audit committee. In contrast, Figure 7.2 shows a **two-tier board system**, as exemplified by Germany's. In a two-tier structure, a supervisory board elects and dismisses members of a management board which makes the major managerial decisions. In both types of boards, shareholders approve the election of an external auditor to work with the firm's audit committee or supervisory board to audit its financial statements.

In Germany, employees of firms with more than 2,000 employees have half of the seats on the supervisory board, although in tie votes the deciding power goes to members elected by shareholders. With firms of 500–2,000 employees, employees have a third of the seats on the board. This employee representation system, with its two-tier board, is known as **co-determination** and is characteristic of Germany and certain other European countries to different degrees. It is a system which indicates an

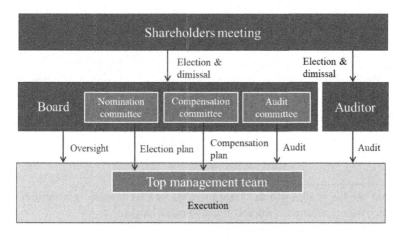

Figure 7.1   One-tier board structure.

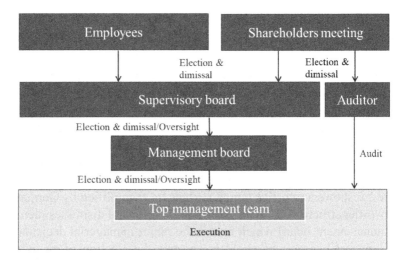

Figure 7.2 Two-tier board structure.

interest in employee protection. France offers both the one-tier and two-tier options, but firms with at least 1,000 employees domestically or 5,000 globally must appoint one employee to the board of directors, or two to boards of eight persons or more.[8] Employee-elected members have a mostly advisory function, however.[9]

Japan has a one-tier board structure, with some variations, but none of its options offer a mechanism for employee representation. This lack is mitigated somewhat by the fact that board members are typically employees promoted under a lifetime employment system. The traditional corporate format is a one-tier board with a parallel board of statutory auditors charged with monitoring management. The latter board comprises at least three members, at least half independent, who are elected at the shareholders' meeting. It has no authority to elect members of the board of directors, unlike the supervisory board under the two-tier system.

A variation of the one-tier board structure, without a board of statutory auditors, was introduced in 2003, followed by another variation

---

[8]Section 184, Loi n° 2019-486 du 22 mai 2019 relative à la croissance et la transformation des enterprises (Business Growth and Transformation Law).

[9]Dammann, J. and Eidenmüller, H. (2021). Codetermination: A poor fit for U.S. corporations. *Columbia Business Law Review*, 2020(3), 870–941.

in 2015. The former is close to the U.S. format in requiring three committees — audit, compensation, and nomination — each having a majority of independent directors. The latter is designed to facilitate a transition from the traditional format, replacing the board of statutory auditors with an audit committee dominated by independent directors. By 2021 the format had been adopted by 34.2 percent of listed firms, indicating its wide acceptance.[10]

2.2. Ownership structure

Corporate governance is strongly affected by the **ownership structure** of a firm. There is a spectrum of share ownership across countries, and the degree of ownership concentration differs markedly among major economies. Ownership of shares is dispersed in the U.S. and the U.K., while being relatively concentrated in continental Europe. The ownership share of the three largest shareholders is 60.2 percent in France and 56.8 percent in Germany, compared with 30.5 percent in the U.S. and 31.9 percent in the U.K. Japan has a dispersed structure that resembles those of the U.S. and the U.K., with a corresponding ownership share of 32.5 percent.[11] A more concentrated family or government ownership is traditionally observed in Asian countries other than Japan.[12]

Despite the persistence of **cross-shareholding** in Japan, where affiliates in a corporate group may create block holdings, the general phenomenon of dispersed ownership underlies an increased interest in the protection of institutional investors as minority shareholders. The country's corporate governance code, and its guideline regarding mergers and acquisitions published in 2019, recommend that conflicted transactions by controlling shareholders and managers be dealt with by establishing an independent committee and obtaining third-party opinions on the fairness of the valuation of such transactions.[13]

---

[10]Tokyo Stock Exchange (2021). Appointment of independent directors and establishment of nomination/remuneration committees by TSE-listed companies, August 2, 2021.

[11]Aminadav, G. and Papaioannou, E. (2020). Corporate control around the world. *Journal of Finance*, 75(3), 1191–1246.

[12]Claessens, S., Djankov, S, and Lang, L. H. P. (2000). The separation of ownership and control in East Asian Corporations. *Journal of Financial Economics*, 58(1–2), 81–112.

[13]Ministry of Economy, Trade and Industry (METI) of Japan (2019). Fair M&A guidelines: Enhancing corporate value and securing shareholders' interests, June 28, 2019.

In contrast, France, Italy, and Germany have a distinctively concentrated form of ownership. It is not uncommon for firms in these countries to be controlled by founder families. Government often has a significant stake in firms and influences the direction of their management. The French government, for example, has an interest in key strategic industries. Firms in these countries also tend to have a stronger employee involvement in management, as seen in the two-tiered board structure in Germany and France, compared to other countries with a one-tier structure.

One of the drivers of the debate over corporate governance structure derives from comparative research by Rafael La Porta *et al.*, who find that common-law jurisdictions, which have relatively stronger protections for minority shareholders, tend to have larger capital markets and economies with dispersed ownership, while civil-law jurisdictions, which have relatively weaker protections, tend to have concentrated share ownership and smaller capital markets and economies.[14] As we have seen, corporate governance structure differs across countries, and the research indicates that policymakers need to consider the impact of corporate governance design on their countries' economic performance.

The validity of the research has been debated over the years with inconclusive results. Contradictory findings have been submitted, such as one which found that civil-law countries experienced stronger economic growth in the first half of the 20th century than common-law countries,[15] and that Japan's introduction of stronger protections for minority shareholders coincided not with dispersed, but more concentrated, ownership in the latter half of the century.[16] However, the research by La Porta *et al.* is significant in that it ignited interest in comparative research into corporate governance structure and its relevance to economic performance.

---

[14]La Porta, R., Lopez-de-Silanes, F., Shleifer, A., and Vishny, R. W. (1997). Legal determinants of external finance. *Journal of Finance*, 52(3), 1131–1150; La Porta, R., Lopez-de-Silanes, F., Shleifer, A., and Vishny, R. W. (1998). Law and finance. *Journal of Political Economy*, 106(6), 1113–1155; La Porta, R., Lopez-de-Silanes, F., Shleifer, A., and Vishny, R. W. (2002). Investor protection and corporate valuation. *Journal of Finance*, 57(3), 1147–1170.

[15]Rajan, R. G. and Zingales, L. (2003). The great reversals: The politics of financial development in the twentieth century. *Journal of Financial Economics*, 69(1), 5–50.

[16]Franks, J., Mayer, C., and Miyajima, H. (2014). The ownership of Japanese corporations in the 20th century. *Review of Financial Studies*, 27(9), 2580–2625.

2.3. Board design

Let us take a closer look at boards. Board members elected at shareholders' meetings have the power to make key decisions on matters including the appointment and dismissal of top managers; mergers and acquisitions; and corporate reorganizations. Most day-to-day decisions are delegated to top managers, but the board has the duty to monitor them. As an institutional mechanism designed to monitor management and protect the interests of shareholders, a board is predicated on the separation of ownership and control. It is the shareholders who approve the election of a board's members and ultimately bear its costs. This means the board's function is self-regulatory, like that of an auditor, with the firm paying it to monitor whether it is being run as its shareholders expect, and without burdening regulators or general taxpayers with the cost of achieving that objective.

While boards are a key characteristic of firms based on the separation of ownership and control, their composition varies across countries. In the U.S., most board members are **independent outside directors**. In 2021, independent outside directors made up 86 percent of the directors of the S&P 500 firms.[17] Industry expertise is often the most important factor in selecting independent outside directors. This is particularly the case when the firm is a startup selecting its first one, as the founder or CEO of a startup is typically responsible for identifying potential candidates.[18] Compare this with Japan, whereas of 2021, 32 percent of the boards of firms listed on the Tokyo Stock Exchange were independent outside directors.[19] This is in line with the country's corporate governance code, which requires, on a comply-or-explain basis, that at least two members, or a third of the board's members where necessary, be independent.[20]

There are growing calls for more **diversity** in board composition. Globally, the percentage of women on boards was 19.7 percent in 2021.[21] The figures were 23.9 percent for the U.S., 30.1 percent for the U.K.,

[17]Spencer Stuart (2021). 2021 U.S. Spencer Stuart Board Index.
[18]Larcker, D. F. and Tayan, B. (2020). The first outside director. Rock Center for Corporate Governance at Stanford University Closer Look Series, No. CGRP-83, 2020.
[19]Tokyo Stock Exchange (2021). Appointment of independent directors and establishment of nomination/remuneration committees by TSE-listed companies, August 2, 2021.
[20]Tokyo Stock Exchange (2021). Japan's corporate governance code: Seeking sustainable corporate growth and increased corporate value over the mid- to long-term, June 11, 2021.
[21]Deloitte Touche Tohmatsu (2022). Women in the boardroom: A global perspective, 7th ed.

28.9 percent for Germany, 43.2 percent for France, and 8.2 percent for Japan.[22] Significantly, in 2019, all the S&P 500 firms had at least one female director.[23]

Institutional investors and proxy advisors tend to vote against boards with little gender diversity. There is a growing trend, particularly in the U.S., to call for greater racial diversity as well. BlackRock, the world's largest institutional investor, asks U.S. firms to have at least two female board members;[24] State Street Global Advisors typically votes against boards with no female directors;[25] and Institutional Shareholder Services (ISS), a proxy advisor, since 2020 has recommended voting against the chairs of nominating and governance committees of firms that have no women on their boards.[26] Glass Lewis sets a higher standard, requiring that there be two women board members in the U.S. and one in Japan, and that women comprise 30 percent of the board in Germany, 33 percent in the U.K., and 40 percent in France.[27] Goldman Sachs announced in 2021 that it would not take companies public in the U.S. or Europe if they did not have at least two diverse board directors. Citing the stronger performance of firms with female directors, it further required that one of these must be a woman.[28] Nasdaq introduced in 2021 a rule to require listed firms to have at least two diverse board members or explain why they did not.[29]

On a state level, California passed legislation in 2018 requiring a minimum of three female directors by the end of 2021 for state-based

---

[22] Financial Services Agency of Japan (2020). The roles and diversity of boards, November 18, 2020.

[23] Fuhrmans, V. (2019). The last all-male board on the S&P 500 is no longer. *Wall Street Journal*, June 24, 2019.

[24] BlackRock (2022). Investment stewardship: Our approach to engagement on board quality and effectiveness, February 2022.

[25] State Street Global Advisors (2021). Proxy voting and engagement guidelines, March 2021.

[26] Institutional Shareholder Services (2021). Proxy voting guidelines, Benchmark policy recommendations, United States, February 1, 2021.

[27] Glass Lewis (2022). 2022 Policy guidelines: United States; Japan; Germany; United Kingdom; France.

[28] Goldman Sachs (2021). Board diversity initiative, July 2021.

[29] The U.S. Securities and Exchange Commission (2021). Self-regulatory organizations; The Nasdaq Stock Market LLC; Order approving proposed rule changes, as modified by amendments No. 1, to adopt listing rules to board diversity and to offer certain listed companies access to a complimentary board recruiting service. Release No. 34-92590.

firms with six or more directors, resulting in an increase in female directors from 17.4 to 27.6 percent over the three years.[30] It also introduced legislation in 2020 requiring firms headquartered in the state to have at least one director from a minority community by 2021, two by 2022 for boards with five to eight people, and three for those with nine or more.[31] The latter legislation was suspended in 2022, however, after a successful court challenge.

2.4. Dealing with misconduct

Along with the monitoring function of boards, the term "corporate governance" is often associated with the occurrence or prevention of accounting fraud, embezzlement, or other forms of corporate misconduct. This reflects the fact that corporate governance reform has often been triggered by the collapse of a large firm.

In the U.K., for instance, the Cadbury report of 1992 was preceded by the bankruptcies of Maxwell Communications and Bank of Credit and Commerce International (BCCI). Continental Europe also experienced the collapse of Parmalat, the Italian dairy food giant, in 2003. In the U.S., the failures of Enron and WorldCom led to the **Sarbanes–Oxley Act** of 2002, which requires that the audit committees of listed firms be composed only of independent outside directors and lays the foundation for **internal controls** employed to date.[32] The act also requires firms to disclose whether the committee has at least one financial expert.[33] The global financial crisis of 2008 was followed by the **Dodd–Frank Act** of 2010, which mandated the independence of all members of compensation committees

---

[30]Senate Bill, No. 826 (SB 826), an act to add Sections 301.3 and 2115.5 to the Corporations Code, relating to corporations, September 30, 2018; Marced, D. (2021). Q1 2021 Equilar Gender Diversity Index, May 20, 2021.

[31]Assembly Bill, No. 979 (AB 979), an act to amend Section 301.3 of, and to add Sections 301.4 and 2115.6 to, the Corporations Code, relating to corporations, September 30, 2020.

[32]Section 301, the Public Company Accounting Reform and Investor Protection Act of 2002 (the Sarbanes–Oxley Act).

[33]Section 407, the Public Company Accounting Reform and Investor Protection Act of 2002 (the Sarbanes–Oxley Act).

and introduced a **say-on-pay** rule.[34] In Japan, accounting fraud by Olympus in 2011 and Toshiba in 2015 prompted the introduction of the corporate governance code in the latter year.

In general, a board is responsible for implementing and monitoring a system designed to identify and deal with risk within an enterprise risk management system that is reviewed at the board level. Under U.S. case law, boards are protected by the business judgment rule as long as they maintain and review this system to ensure its legal and regulatory compliance.[35] **Disclosure** requirements complement these internal controls under the principle that sunlight is the best disinfectant.[36]

Neither directors nor public investors have effective means of uncovering efforts by top managers or employees to hide or even falsify information. Thus, **whistleblowing** is built into the internal control system as a way to mitigate intentional asymmetries of information. The Dodd–Frank Act reinforced the protection of whistleblowers by establishing a system of monetary awards,[37] ranging from 10 to 30 percent of the monetary sanctions collected by the government; the government was mindful that it was a whistleblower who revealed the accounting fraud at Enron. Given developments in information technology such as smartphones and social media, the hurdles for whistleblowing seem to be lowering both technically and psychologically, blurring the traditional corporate boundaries for revealing misconduct.

For firms, however, building and maintaining effective internal controls, as well as meeting enhanced disclosure requirements, come with significant costs. These costs are ultimately borne by shareholders. They include the direct costs of running an organization with such systems in place, including the staff and technology to prepare, audit, and file disclosure materials, and the indirect costs of opening themselves up to potential competition from rivals accessing the information they disclose. Private firms may choose to remain so for as long as possible, while public firms may decide to go private. In an environment where the value of the

---

[34] Sections 951 and 952, the Dodd–Frank Wall Street Reform and Consumer Protection Act (the Dodd–Frank Act).

[35] In re Caremark International Inc. Derivative Litigation, 698 A.2d 959 (Del. Ch. 1996).

[36] Brandeis, L. (1914). *Other People's Money and How the Bankers Use It*. New York, NY: Frederick A. Stokes.

[37] Section 922, the Dodd–Frank Wall Street Reform and Consumer Protection Act (the Dodd–Frank Act).

intangible assets represented by information is more important than ever, firms are increasingly desiring to remain or go private not only for cost considerations but also for competitive ones.[38]

Motives like these are supported by growth in private equity funds, venture capital funds, and other forms of private capital. However, the whole private capital market is not deep enough to absorb all the capital requirements of currently listed firms. In any case, as these funds typically require liquidity at some point because of the limited life of their sources, they provide only a transitory solution. To continue to fund their growth, therefore, most firms, particularly large ones, have to live with the requirements of internal control and disclosure.

2.5. Self-assessment

Given that a board is a built-in mechanism for monitoring management for the sake of shareholders at their own cost, the question arises as to who will monitor the board. Instead of creating a chain of "watchers of watchers," whose total costs would exceed their benefits, board members conduct self-assessments of their own performance, often by bringing in third-party consultants.

This need for self-assessment also pertains to the election of board members at shareholders' meetings. Since candidates for shareholder approval are nominated by a committee composed of board members, the committee members are essentially proposing to elect themselves. From this perspective, the requirement for self-assessment is also a built-in mechanism for maintaining the quality and transparency of the board, both to protect shareholders and to offer a groundwork for the process of approving board elections.

3. Conflicts of Interest

3.1. Management entrenchment

An effective board that monitors management can foster firm performance that benefits shareholders. Despite this monitoring, however, the

---

[38] Stulz, R. M. (2020). Public versus private equity. *Oxford Review of Economic Policy*, 36(2), 275–290.

interests of management may diverge from those of shareholders, as managers may favor themselves at the shareholders' expense. From this perspective, researchers have measured the degree of **management entrenchment** attempted by managers and associated it with firm value.

A notable example is an index constructed by Paul Gompers *et al.*[39] Known as the **G-index** after *governance*, this consists of 24 factors relating to the protection of shareholders' rights. These factors include provisions in articles of incorporation, such as anti-takeover provisions, golden parachutes, classified boards, limitations on charter and bylaw amendments that favor managers over shareholders, and a supermajority requirement for mergers and acquisitions which raises the bar for changes of control. These provisions are conducive to management entrenchment at the expense of shareholders. The index also reflects shareholder protections in state laws, such as a rule designed to prevent price discrimination by limiting bid prices in two-tier offers, and another requiring majority approval by disinterested shareholders for an acquirer to effectuate voting rights on purchased shares. Interestingly, the authors find that shares with stronger shareholder protection outperform those whose protection is weaker.

Another index, devised by Lucian Bebchuk *et al.*, is called the **E-index** after *entrenchment*.[40] It narrows down the 24 factors adopted by the G-index, which they view as overlapping, down to six, including provisions on golden parachutes, staggered boards, poison pills, and the supermajority requirement for mergers and charter amendments. They similarly show that firm value correlates negatively with the degree of management entrenchment, and correlates positively with strong shareholder protection.

3.1.1. Compensation

Compensation design for managers is a key factor in corporate governance where the interests of managers and shareholders may diverge. Managers may try to pay themselves excessive amounts in the face of

---

[39]Gompers, P. A., Ishii, J. L., and Metrick, A. (2003). Corporate governance and equity prices. *Quarterly Journal of Economics*, 118(1), 107–155.
[40]Bebchuk, L., Cohen, A., and Ferrell, A. (2009). What matters in corporate governance? *Review of Financial Studies*, 22(2), 783–827.

shareholder opposition. A compensation package generally consists of a cash payment along with stock-related compensation such as restricted stocks and stock options with certain vesting periods. Cash payments are often contingent on such aspects of financial performance as annual earnings and total shareholder return (TSR), especially for top managers with extensive control over the firm.

Both compensation and its composition show differences across countries. Figure 7.3 compares compensation among U.S., European, and Japanese CEOs.[41] While there is a distinct difference in the absolute amount of total compensation, its composition differs as well. For instance, U.S. managers receive 74 percent of their compensation in the form of long-term incentives such as restricted stocks and stock options, whereas German, U.K., and French managers receive 41 percent, 48 percent, and 39 percent of their compensation in that form. The ratio for Japanese managers is only 27 percent. Ratios of fixed basic compensation are in the opposite order: 42 percent for Japanese managers, 31 percent,

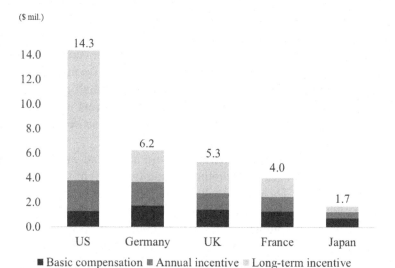

Figure 7.3 Compensation packages.

Source: Willis Towers Watson (2021). CEO pay landscape in Japan, the U.S., and Europe — 2021 analysis, July 29, 2021.

---

[41] Willis Towers Watson (2021). CEO pay landscape in Japan, the U.S. and Europe — 2021 analysis, July 29, 2021.

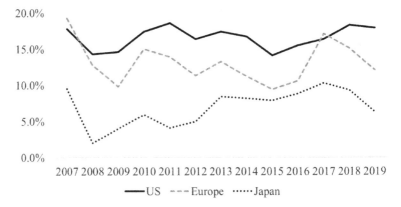

Figure 7.4 Return on equity.

Source: Ministry of Economy, Trade and Industry of Japan (METI) (2021). Study on long-term management and investment for sustainable value creation, May 31, 2021.

27 percent, and 28 percent for French, U.K., and German managers respectively, and a mere 9 percent for managers in the U.S.

Differences in compensation might also reflect divergent cultural attitudes toward pecuniary rewards and equality within organizations. While a large pay gap in absolute terms can strongly incentivize managers, it can also have an adverse effect on employee morale. A small gap may relate to the emphasis on job security seen in Japanese firms and to a lesser extent in European firms, and may help maintain a sense of workplace engagement as well.

The discrepancies seem generally in line with those in financial performance. Figure 7.4 shows the return on equity (ROE) of U.S., European and Japanese firms. The order of shareholder value creation, as measured by ROE, coincides with managers' compensation level and the degree of emphasis on stock compensation. This is consistent with the view that stock compensation literally makes managers into owners invested in the future growth of their firm. It is not a coincidence that Japan's emphasis on improving shareholder return occurs in parallel with pay reforms emphasizing stock compensation and performance-based awards.[42]

---

[42]Ministry of Economy, Trade and Industry (METI) of Japan (2020). Executive compensation for proactive management: A guide to the introduction of incentive plans for sustainable corporate growth, September 30, 2020.

3.1.2. *Say on pay*

The differences in compensation also reflect each country's norms and institutional arrangements regarding shareholder control over executive compensation. In the U.S., shareholders only have non-binding voting rights over compensation, even if they believe it is excessive. The Dodd–Frank Act of 2010 empowers shareholders of U.S. firms to take part in advisory voting in addition to obtaining information on executive compensation, known as **say on pay**.[43] Under the legislation, firms must disclose compensation for executives and hold non-binding shareholder votes to approve their compensation programs. Shareholders also vote at least once every six years on the frequency of such advisory votes, the longest interval being three years. Although these votes are non-binding, the rates at which compensation is approved may affect managers' decisions in the following years.

Oversight by boards also serves to protect shareholders in this regard. Compensation is approved by a compensation committee consisting of independent outside directors, but a trend toward emphasizing shareholder approval suggests that committee approval has limited restraining power over compensation levels. This is partly because the frequent practice of referring to compensation benchmarks provided by outside consultants in making these approvals may have a ratcheting effect when managers seek at least the same level of compensation as their industry peers.[44] More fundamentally, however, the weakness of the restraining power is inevitable given that committee members set their own compensation as well as that of their top managers, and that it is often these same top managers who decide which candidates for independent outside directorships will be presented for approval at shareholders' meetings.

Germany, which maintains a high level of compensation relative to other European nations, in 2009 added a non-binding say-on-pay provision to its corporate law.[45] In contrast, the U.K., where non-binding voting was originally adopted in 2002, amended its law in 2013 to make such

---

[43] Section 951(a) (Executive Compensation), the Dodd–Frank Wall Street Reform and Consumer Protection Act (the Dodd–Frank Act).

[44] Jochem, T., Ormazabal, G., and Rajamani, A. (2020). Why have CEO pay levels become less diverse? ECGI Working Paper Series in Finance, No. 707/2020.

[45] Tröger, T. H. and Walz, U. (2019). Does say on pay matter? Evidence from Germany. *European Company and Financial Law Review*, 16(3), 381–414; Vesper-Gräske, M.

votes binding, though only for matters of compensation policy.[46] France followed suit in 2018 by legislating a binding say-on-pay vote for compensation policy and part of compensation that is contingent on performance as well.[47]

Japanese corporate law is the most stringent in requiring that the total amount of directors' compensation, and the content of their performance-based compensation, be approved by a majority of shareholder votes based on the disclosure of an individual compensation policy approved by the board of directors.[48]

While research shows that the effects of binding voting tend to be only marginally significant in lowering pay,[49] these differences reflect the norms prevailing in each country. These norms and institutional arrangements may shift over time, influenced by shareholders seeking similar performance and protection across different jurisdictions, or still persist, as seen in the continued emphasis on stakeholder value in Japan.

3.1.3. Dual stock

Another place where we see concern over management entrenchment is in the design of corporate stock issues. **Dual stock** is a stock structure that differentiates voting rights among different classes of stock. Typically, the class of shares owned by public investors carries one vote per share, while the class owned by specific individuals, such as the firm's founders, carries more than one, most commonly ten, votes per share. This is a deviation from the one-share, one-vote principle that is the general rule among corporations. The principle is based on the view that control rights should be proportionate to the economic risk assumed by shareholders in terms of capital contribution. Firms adopting such a dual structure include

---

(2013). "Say on pay" in Germany: The regulatory framework and empirical evidence. *German Law Journal*, 14(7), 749–795.

[46]Section 439, the Companies Act of 2006; Wu, B., MacNeil, I, and Chalaczkiewicz-Ladna, K. (2020). "Say on pay" regulations and director remuneration: Evidence from the UK in the past two decades. *Journal of Corporate Law Studies*, 20(2), 541–577.

[47]Pietrancosta, A. (2017). Say on pay: The new French legal regime in light of the Shareholders' Rights Directive II. *Colloque*, RTDF No. 3- 2017, pp. 105–109.

[48]Section 361, the Companies Act.

[49]Correa, R. and Lel, U. (2016). Say on pay laws, executive compensation, pay slice, and firm valuation around the world. *Journal of Financial Economics*, 122(3), 500–520.

Alphabet, Meta Platforms (Facebook), Dell, and Palantir. At these firms, founders and other specific individuals retain a disproportionate share of voting rights even while issuing additional shares to fund growth, as other structures might dilute their ownership and voting rights.

Firms with a dual stock structure are shown to have outperformed those without one in the 2010s, particularly in the years immediately after the initial public offering.[50] However, we also know that until the 2000s, a dual-stock structure led to a decline in firm value[51] and was associated with higher CEO pay, worse acquisitions, and poorer investment decisions.[52] In terms of a causal relationship, however, it may be the case that growing firms with strong bargaining power tend to adopt a dual stock structure, rather than the structure itself resulting in strong performance.

Institutional investors are generally opposed to the idea of weighted controlling rights. Some academics argue for limiting use of the structure, by mandating a sunset clause, for example, under which it would automatically be unwound after a certain period, such as ten years, with shareholder approval required for extensions.[53] This also prevents such special stocks from being handed over to someone not intended at the outset. A breakthrough clause has also been proposed, by which the structure is unwound when a certain threshold of listed shares is acquired by a third party.

Opposition to the structure is also seen among some stock index providers whose major customers are institutional investors. Standard and Poor's (S&P) announced in 2017 that they would not include firms with a dual stock structure in their premier S&P 500 stock index.[54] Grandfathering was provided, however, to keep existing firms such as Alphabet and Meta Platforms (Facebook) in the index. Other major index providers, such as MSCI, did not follow suit. The threat of exclusion from

---

[50] Ahn, B. H., Fisch, J. E., Patatoukas, P. N., and Davidoff Solomon, S. (2021). Synthetic governance. *Columbia Business Law Review*, 2021(2), 476–519.

[51] Gompers, P. A., Ishii, J., and Metrick, A. (2010). Extreme governance: An analysis of dual-class firms in the United States. *Review of Financial Studies*, 23(3), 1051–1088.

[52] Masulis, R. W., Wang, C., and Xie, F. (2009). Agency problems at dual-class companies. *Journal of Finance*, 64(4), 1697–1727.

[53] Bebchuk, L. A. and Kastiel, K. (2017). The untenable case for perpetual dual-class stock, *Virginia Law Review*, 103(4), 585–631.

[54] S&P Global (2017). S&P Dow Jones Indices announces decision on multi-class shares and voting rules, July 31, 2017.

the indices may work, in that inclusion in a widely adopted index is prestigious and may spark a rally in stock prices by necessitating that index investors track it to purchase their shares. This effect lasts only in the short run, however, and inclusion is not always beneficial in that it is found that firms that are added to a stock index tend to increase their share repurchases thereafter, presumably to match their peers in the index, while decreasing their investments and showing a lower return on assets.[55]

While a dual stock structure can give managers wide discretion, and possibly lead to management entrenchment, it may also provide managers with insulation from short-term pressure by investors. For instance, if managers want to take a long-term approach focusing on research and development, while investors want immediate, short-term returns with payouts, the founders' controlling rights will safeguard their interests from such an interruption. However, the motive of founders in holding on to their controlling rights may merely be to secure the unique benefits that come with management entrenchment, against which shareholders have little means to intervene under a dual structure. Investors, meanwhile, will continue to invest in these firms if their financial performance is too attractive to pass up. The dual structure stands on an intricate balance of bargaining power between managers wanting control and shareholders wanting protection.

3.2. Conflicted transactions

Conflicts of interest also arise in one-off transactions, as well as in such recurring issues as compensation and voting power design. These **related-party transactions** are observed in capital transactions such as **buyouts** where controlling shareholders acquire shares from minority shareholders or **management buyouts (MBOs)** where managers and their partner investors acquire shares from other shareholders.

In these cases, the controlling shareholders or managers have an incentive to acquire shares at a low price; the seller shareholders want the opposite, creating an obvious conflict of interest. Without an appropriate mechanism to protect them, minority shareholders are at a disadvantage in that their minority position means they have inferior information and

---

[55]Bennett, B., Stulz, R. M., and Wang, Z. (2020). Does joining the S&P 500 index hurt firms? NBER Working Paper, No. 27593.

less bargaining power than controlling shareholders and managers. If would-be minority shareholders have concerns about being denied fair treatment during a change of control, they will be unwilling to invest in fear of potential exploitation.

Some shareholder protection mechanisms are designed to mitigate this concern by providing visibility and predictability for dispersed investors. Major avenues for this purpose are to oblige buyers to be sufficiently transparent with sellers regarding information on transactions and fair valuation of shares, and to establish impartial processes by requiring that transactions be approved by an independent committee. A notable example of such a mechanism is a series of judicial standards established by the Delaware Supreme Court in the U.S. as to when managers in a conflicted transaction are to be granted discretion under the business judgment rule. Transactions can be classified on the basis of whether controlling shareholders are conflicted or, in the absence of controlling shareholders, whether managers are conflicted.

3.2.1. Transactions involving controlling shareholders

In cases where **controlling shareholders** are conflicted by being involved on both sides of a transaction or expecting to receive unique benefits from it, the court requires management to establish *before* any negotiations begin that their final decision will be subject to approval by both (a) an independent and disinterested special committee of board members *and* (b) a majority of minority shareholders. The latter is called the **majority of minority (MoM)** requirement. These approvals must be observed in order for management to be granted the benefit of discretion under the **business judgment rule**.[56]

If management fails to follow this process, the court lifts its judicial standards from those applied under the business judgment rule and examines the entire fairness of the transaction in regard to fair pricing and fair dealing. This is called the **entire fairness standard**,[57] and means that controlling shareholders and managers are more likely to be held responsible for any unfairness in the terms and conditions of the conflicted transaction. However, if management, *after* the start of negotiations, goes

---

[56]Kahn v. M&F Worldwide Corp., 88 A.3d 635 (Del. 2014).
[57]Weinberger v. UOP, Inc. 457 A.2d 701 (Del. 1984).

through the process of obtaining the approval of an independent and disinterested special committee *or* a majority of minority shareholders, they are less likely to be held responsible, since the **burden of proof** regarding the transaction's fairness as a whole shift from the directors to the plaintiffs, who may be minority shareholders claiming that the transaction is unfair.[58]

This process-related requirement for approval by an independent committee and a majority of minority shareholders mitigates issues arising from conflicts of interest, and the courts tend to closely look at specific factual processes that firms follow in choosing to apply judicial standards.

3.2.2. Transactions not involving controlling shareholders

In cases not involving controlling shareholders, there may be problems if the **managers** involved in a conflicted transaction seek to benefit themselves at the expense of dispersed shareholders. In such cases, there are other requirements that limit managerial discretion under a different case law. Specifically, if either (a) less than half of the board's members are independent and disinterested, indicating that the board is deferential to managers, or (b) the transaction involves a change of control or the firm has anti-takeover protections in place, indicating that the managers are conflicted and prone to entrenchment, the court will require approval by a majority of *fully informed* and *uncoerced* shareholders in order for management to have the benefit of discretion under the business judgment rule.[59] In the absence of such approval under full information and an uncoercive structure, the court will again apply the entire fairness standard to the transaction rather than granting managers wide discretion under the business judgment rule.

Coercion of shareholders typically occurs under a **two-tier offer** for shares, when managers and their partner investors set a lower price at the second step than at the first. This gives shareholders an incentive to surrender their holdings at the first step, lest they be squeezed out at a lower price at the second step — something that is possible only if the acquirer succeeds in collecting sufficient shares at the first step, enabling it to

---

[58]Kahn v. Lynch Communications Systems, Inc. 638 A.2d 1110 (Del. 1994).
[59]Corwin v. KKR Financial Holdings LLC, 125 A.3d 304 (Del. 2015).

squeeze out the remaining, dissenting minority shareholders. This pressures, or coerces, the shareholders into surrendering their shares at the first step, thus completing the cycle and enabling managers and their partner investors to succeed in gathering the votes they need. The courts tread cautiously around offer structures involving price discrimination, and tend to view them as coercive. In response, firms often offer the same price at both steps, in which case there is no such pressure and shareholders are able to focus on the fairness of a single offered price in making their decisions.

Under a doctrine requiring fully informed and uncoerced approval for transactions involving an insufficiently independent board or a change in control, shareholder approval is of prime importance in "cleansing" board-level conflicts and mitigating a board's deference toward managers at the expense of shareholders. Moreover, obtaining the approval of the majority of shareholders discharges a board from the Revlon duties,[60] which, in requiring that board directors pay fiduciary duties to maximize shareholder value when deciding on a firm's sale, explicitly put the interests of shareholders before the self-interest of managers.

Under the requirement for full information and lack of coercion, it is often the case that shareholders file a lawsuit claiming that they were not fully informed about the offer, even if they were not coerced. This is an easy entry point for dissenting shareholders, because "full information" is inherently hard to achieve given the asymmetric information held by firms and shareholders. Here, however, there is the danger of litigation abuse by opportunistic investors aiming to settle with the firm for extra payment by involving the court. In response, the Delaware court raised the bar in 2016 by making it more difficult for plaintiffs to win lawsuits that seek only greater disclosure without any meaningful benefits.[61]

3.2.3. Summary

What these case laws indicate in common is that process-wise, the protection of shareholders ultimately boils down to requiring their approval. When a transaction involves controlling shareholders, approval is required from minority shareholders. And when no controlling shareholders are

---

[60]Revlon, Inc. v. MacAndrews & Forbes Holdings, Inc., 506 A.2d 173 (Del. 1986).
[61]In re Trulia, Inc. Stockholder Litigation, 129 A.3d 884, 899 (Del. Ch. 2016).

involved, but the board lacks independence, approval is required from dispersed shareholders who are fully informed and uncoerced. Such mechanisms are essential if potential shareholders are to feel comfortable that their interests will be properly protected, even if they have only a minority stake and less-than-superior access to information.

The laws also show that board independence is a key component in determining whether managers should be granted wide discretion. The more independent the board, the more discretion granted to management; otherwise, shareholders, or the courts, will have a greater say in judging the fairness of managerial decisions. This emphasis on the board relates back to the issue of board design. Given that it is primarily the board that approves such transactions and owes fiduciary duties to shareholders in making such decisions, board composition matters in terms of shareholder protection and confidence in managers. This is why board design is a matter of keen interest to shareholders, particularly institutional investors, and proxy advisors.

4. Proxy Advisors and Activism

4.1. *Proxy advisors*

In light of the asymmetry of information held by managers and shareholders, protecting shareholders from management entrenchment is key to the structuring of good corporate governance. Institutional investors are paying increasing attention to aspects of corporate governance that define their rights as shareholders, often as minority ones. In addition, shareholders are pressing managers for better protection by demonstrating their approval or disapproval through their votes at shareholders' meetings, even while knowing that their individual votes are unlikely to override management proposals.

Indicating the importance of voting decisions and their results, **proxy advisory firms**, such as ISS and Glass Lewis, are exerting a growing influence in that their recommendations for or against management proposals are affecting the actual voting decisions of shareholders. These proxy advisors publish country- and region-specific guidelines for their recommendations that reflect differences in institutional and regulatory environments and practices across jurisdictions. They place emphasis on matters such as board independence and diversity, compensation design, payout policy, and anti-takeover defenses that could reinforce management entrenchment. They also pay attention to financial performance, by recommending against voting for the directors of firms that fail to achieve a reasonable financial return for shareholders and show no sign of improvement.

Institutional investors, such as mutual funds, pension funds, and endowments, can exert their influence by voting at shareholders' meetings with a collective voting power that can overturn managers' proposals. However, institutional investors only rarely enhance their influence by coordinating their votes, normally limiting themselves to individual, private communications with firms if any at all. This apparent isolation is because regulations require that collective voting be disclosed in a timely manner in order to prevent groups of investors from attempting to manipulate the market. For example, the U.S. regulation requires that investors disclose the fact of such coordination when the total share of their voting rights exceeds 5 percent.[62]

In addition to regulatory requirements, there exists the classic problem of **collective action** in regard to economic incentives.[63] Investors will be unwilling to take action to increase the value of their holdings if they know they cannot capture all or a substantial part of the benefits that will come with them, and that other investors will enjoy a free ride. With no investors taking action, management will consequently be empowered. Proxy advisors serve to mitigate such problems by pooling research that would otherwise be conducted individually by shareholders, essentially lowering the costs for each, and by indirectly coordinating the votes of shareholders by means of recommendations that give a general direction for voting while not eliciting disclosure requirements. Although ultimate decisions on voting rest with the shareholders themselves, the recommendations of proxy advisors can have a coordinating effect provided they have gained the shareholders' trust.

Mindful of the increasing influence of proxy advisors, the U.S. has debated regulation of their activities.[64] Regulations introduced in 2021 consist mostly of disclosure requirements for conflicts of interest involving these advisors, such as when advice is given to both firms and

---

[62] Sections 240.13d-1 and 13d-101, Chapter 17, Code of Federal Regulation.
[63] Olson, M. (1971). *The Logic of Collective Action: Public Goods and the Theory of Groups, Revised ed.* Cambridge, MA: Harvard University Press.
[64] The U.S. Securities and Exchange Commission (2021). Proxy voting advice. Release No. 34-93595; File No. S7-17-21.

investors. Such regulatory moves reflect the fact that an increase in influence can bring corresponding degree of regulation.

In parallel with the growing influence of proxy advisors, U.S. firms are undergoing a concentration of ownership as well, with the three largest institutional shareholders, namely index funds, holding 24 percent of firms on average, compared to 16 percent in Europe and 8 percent in Japan.[65] Thus their voting decisions also have significant influence and draw attention from other minority shareholders. This leads to similar scrutiny of their behavior, under the argument that despite the passive nature of their design, they should fulfill responsibilities according to their influence and properly monitor their investees, and that otherwise a vacuum of governance would result.[66]

4.2. Activism

Activist funds can be included among the short-term shareholders against whom managers try to insulate themselves, even when facing possible accusations of entrenchment. In contrast to such passive investors as index funds, activist funds often make their proposals public in campaigns designed to exert pressure on management and gather support from other shareholders. This publicity partly alleviates the collective action problem as well, in that other shareholders learn of the activist funds' ideas while the costs are borne only by the activists themselves. Other investors have only to decide whether to agree or disagree with them. To capture the greatest benefits possible, activist funds typically accumulate shares of their target firms before launching their campaigns, to which the stock markets often react positively in anticipation of improved value. Their proposals include an increase in dividends and share repurchases, the appointment of new directors recommended by the funds, the divestiture of non-core businesses, and the cancellation of announced plans for mergers and acquisitions. Recent proposals involve stakeholder value as well. Engine No. 1, for example, waged a successful campaign against Exxon Mobil to reduce the energy giant's carbon footprint, gaining three

---

[65]OECD (2021). The future of corporate governance in capital markets following the COVID-19 crisis, June 30, 2021.
[66]Bebchuk, L. and Hirst, S. (2019). Index funds and the future of corporate governance: Theory, evidence, and policy. *Columbia Law Review*, 119(8), 2029–2146.

board seats with support from public pension funds and index investors.[67]

When facing an activist campaign, managers need to defend their own plans and secure backing from the board. If a campaign succeeds in obtaining support from other shareholders, managers may find it hard to resist the activists' proposals and be forced to switch their course of action to accommodate them, thus losing managerial credibility. Shareholders, including other activist funds, that support proposals by an activist fund may form a loosely connected shareholders group called a "wolf pack," which acquires shares and engages with firms in parallel without invoking the disclosure requirement for collective action.[68] Faced with the threat of a public face-off, a firm may opt to compromise through private negotiations with an activist fund even before the launching of a campaign. Such compromises may include increasing payouts to shareholders and accepting one or two board members in return for the withdrawal of other demands. Indeed, there is evidence in the U.K. that behind-the-scenes tactics prove more effective than public campaigns.[69]

Activist funds usually are not looking for full or majority control. Rather, they find it sufficient to have a certain share of ownership, typically less than 10 percent, which enables them to be heard. This is different from the traditional market notion of corporate control which assumes a full takeover, where managers are spurred into imposing discipline by the fear that inefficiency could lay a firm open to a takeover.[70] The relatively low level of ownership is not only for the practical reason that the market capitalization of prominent firms, which can be worth tens or even hundreds of billions of dollars, far exceeds the several billion which is the usual size of an activist fund, but also because the funds' demands — such as for more short-run payouts that would do more to win them support from other public investors than proposals of strategic, complex decisions

---

[67]Phillips, M. (2021). Exxon's board defeat signals the rise of social-good activists. *New York Times*, June 9, 2021.

[68]Coffee, J. C. and Palia, D. (2016). The wolf pack at the door: The impact of hedge fund activism on corporate governance. *Journal of Corporation Law*, 41(3), 545–608.

[69]Becht, M., Franks, J., Mayer, C., and Rossi, S. (2009). Returns to shareholder activism: Evidence from a clinical study of the Hermes UK Focus Fund. *Review of Financial Studies*, 22(8), 3093–3129.

[70]Manne, H. G. (1965). Mergers and the market for corporate control. *Journal of Political Economy*, 73(2), 110–120.

on which different investors might disagree — are more or less boilerplate among firms. This strategy does not require significant outlays on analysis, either, compared to one tailored to specific target firms.

While activists are criticized for their short-term focus, there is no empirical evidence that shows that activist funds damage long-term value by pursuing short-term value.[71] Rather, when activist funds disclose their holdings in a firm, the firm's stock price is shown to rise by an average of 7 percent without any long-term reversal,[72] indicating that the improvement is sustainable. Further, the innovation level, as measured by patent counts and citations, rises despite the lower expenditures made on research and development.[73] Hence there is a view that activist funds enhance corporate governance through their proposal activities.[74] While their short-term focus and disruptive nature may be undeniable given the limited life of their funds, activists also have a disciplining effect in keeping management entrenchment in check. Policymakers have discussed placing stricter regulations on activist funds, such as requirements for greater disclosure, with a view to protecting firms in their pursuit of long-term value. They are often countered by concerns over the management entrenchment that could result in the absence of such potential pressures.

5. Conclusion

Corporate governance structure is a balancing act. It needs to manage the many places where conflicts arise between managers and shareholders, such as dual stock structure and compensation design, and between controlling and minority shareholders, such as judicial standards over conflicted transactions. The right balance gives rise to confidence in the firms in which shareholders invest their capital; more fundamentally, however, the structured institutional processes which manage these various interests

[71]Bebchuk, L. A., Brav, A., and Jiang, W. (2015). The long-term effects of hedge fund activism. *Columbia Law Review*, 115(5), 1085–1156.

[72]Brav, A., Jiang, W., Partnoy, F., and Thomas, R. (2008). Hedge fund activism, corporate governance, and firm performance. *Journal of Finance*, 63(4), 1729–1775.

[73]Brav, A., Jiang, W., Ma, S., and Tian, X. (2018). How does hedge fund activism reshape corporate innovation? *Journal of Financial Economics*, 130(2), 237–264.

[74]Gilson, R. J. and Gordon, J. N. (2013). The agency costs of agency capitalism: Activist investors and the revaluation of governance rights. *Columbia Law Review*, 113(4), 863–928.

form an indispensable foundation for firms. In particular, recent developments in regulatory design reflect efforts to make the structure more visible and predictable for shareholders, including dispersed, minority shareholders such as institutional investors that are collectively influential. The design of boards with more independence and diversity is the key for this purpose.

Accompanying these developments has been an increase in transparency and formalization that has promoted comparative studies of corporate governance structure across countries. Firms in different countries have different ownership structures, and each firm has its own combination of board design, compensation packages, and accompanying conflicts. These structures and processes will not necessarily converge into one form. But overall they are evolving, in particular toward better protection for shareholders, which seek similar protections across jurisdictions. Firms change, and so do forms. Like the management of firms, the structuring of corporate governance is part of a continuous endeavor to deliver sustained performance.

Conclusion

In concluding the book, let us look over the seven chapters from three key perspectives: the evolution of the corporation, the board, and the financial markets, and find the relationships among them.

1. Evolution of the Corporation

Firms have had a stable corporate format for centuries (Chapter 1). Although a number of variations have emerged, such as the public benefit corporation (Chapter 6), the fact that none are in a position to replace the traditional corporation points to the robustness and dominance of the traditional format. Meanwhile, the global conversation on corporate governance is serving to clarify differences among jurisdictions (Chapter 7), and global mergers and acquisitions are causing individual firms to manage these differences across borders (Chapter 5). Noticing such differences does not necessarily mean eradicating them, but we do see that large institutional investors, such as index funds, own shares in most large firms across jurisdictions (Chapter 5). This may play a part in causing formats to converge, to the extent that such shareholders want equivalent protection in all jurisdictions (Chapter 7).

Nevertheless, form is one thing and substance is another. Adopting the public benefit corporation format, for instance, is not the same as being socially conscious, nor does remaining within the traditional corporation format mean that a firm is irresponsible. Since it is people that give substance to the legal construct of a firm (Introduction), the awareness and vision of managers and investors may matter more than a prescribed legal format. As is the case with legal formats, the evolution of people's ideas and needs leads to changes in laws and regulations, as seen in the standardization of disclosure rules (Chapter 3), reforms in the aftermath of corporate scandals (Chapter 7), and the global conversation on climate change (Chapter 6). These changes also serve as a basis for the activities of firms with different formats.

2. Evolution of the Board

As a board is a group of people, there are many elements to the human interactions that affect corporate decisions. Since 2020 and throughout the pandemic, for example, technology has enabled us to communicate online with others across the world. But the influence of technology is not confined to communications, as human decisions are increasingly aided by data, artificial intelligence, and machines. It will be a long time before machines replace the humans that manage firms and make board decisions, but it is already clear that we rely on machines to a greater or lesser extent in deciding things, even if we meet in boardrooms for the final steps of the process. When layered analyses are presented to a board for capital investment decisions (Chapter 2), with information on the financial markets included (Chapter 3), they are backed by data and machines from the corporate floors.

Legally speaking, boards require natural persons as directors in most jurisdictions (Introduction), except for a rarely adopted case in the U.K. that allows a corporation as a director.[1] Because of this legal requirement, even special purpose vehicles (SPVs) in project finance arrangements have substance in terms of a human presence; otherwise, the corporation's SPV will be denied limited liability (Chapter 4) to the detriment of its sponsors. Technically, the absence of humans on a board makes it difficult to litigate against directors for liability. From a different angle, enabling firms to have machine-only boards would prove unpopular because it would deprive people of jobs, and highly prestigious ones at that. Requiring a human presence also serves to point up the tendencies involved in decision-making, including such behavioral characteristics as

---

[1]Bainbridge, S. M. and Henderson, M. T. (2018). *Outsourcing the Board: How Board Service Providers Can Improve Corporate Governance*. Cambridge, UK: Cambridge University Press.

the overconfidence that appear in mergers and acquisitions decisions (Chapter 5).

As humans on boards are increasingly aided in their decision-making by data and machines, the potential arises for a change in how humans are perceived to function there. Although data security is already a central focus of monitoring by boards (Chapter 7), the role of human directors will increasingly involve more "human" aspects, such as dealing with social justice and fairness and reviewing assumptions on corporate activities that omit the externalities they impose to the detriment of stakeholders and the natural environment (Chapter 6). Recent moves toward carbon neutrality and gender equality, for instance, are key examples of such roles, as machines cannot lead firms to be greener and more gender-equal unless humans work toward those values and change the machines' data inputs.

3. Evolution of Financial Markets

Financial markets, like corporations, are a product of institutional design involving a variety of regulations for the maintenance of transparency and fairness for participants. One of their main objectives in economic terms is to mitigate asymmetric information (Chapter 3). However, one thing we learned from the global financial crisis of 2008 is that financial markets can fail, despite all efforts to keep them working soundly. Also, we still have no systematic means of assessing risk for entities other than regularly operated businesses with a stable cash flow (Chapter 1).

The experience of a crisis like that of 2008 introduces a new set of uncertainties, or even fears, into the markets. While new regulations to strengthen corporate governance were introduced in the aftermath of the crisis (Chapter 7), such as the Dodd–Frank Act in the U.S., these are part of a continuous round of trial and error aimed at maintaining confidence in the markets. A decisive factor enabling expansion of the markets was the invention of limited liability (Chapter 4), which, by according to investors the luxury of being minimally concerned with the possibility of being held liable beyond the amount of their investment, keeps them interested in participating in the markets. A series of regulations on contemporary corporate governance may appear incremental compared to the introduction of limited liability centuries ago, but modern regulatory architecture has a totally different level of sophistication that is geared to the complexities of modern financial markets. Also, the growing integration of financial markets means that global policy coordination, and the political will to implement it, is growing in importance as well.

There is a similar need for further coordination on issues of the disclosure and measurement of stakeholder value through such frameworks as the TCFD and SASB (Chapter 6). Since many key agendas, such as climate change, are of global scale and have large externalities, policy coordination at the disclosure and measurement levels is key to their success. This will be a touchstone for a new era of global coordination, central to the creation of reliable financial markets which improve from generation to generation.

4. Final Words

Firms compete by inventing and developing necessary goods and services, continually changing the world. Firms grow and create value by funding their innovative projects in the financial markets, and human design, expressed through firms, laws, and markets developed over centuries, is what enable us to enjoy the results today. These developments are not static, but dynamic. Financial management and corporate governance are the frameworks through which we view and navigate such dynamics. We hope this book has equipped readers with the perspectives required to make key decisions and find unexplored value in evolving markets.

Index

equity, 16, 24, 30, 41, 44, 64, 66, 72,
  83, 91, 97, 100, 115, 168
equity beta, 92
ESG indices, 162
EU-Japan economic partnership
  agreement, 167
EU Takeover Directive, 128
evaluation, 44, 61, 144
ex ante, 60, 155
exchange, 120
exchange offer, 127
exchange ratio, 121
exit option, 54
expansion option, 54
expectation, 10, 143, 147, 151
ex post, 60, 155
externalities, 144
Exxon Mobil, 159, 190

F
Facebook, 109, 183
Fairchild Semiconductor
  International, 135
fair disclosure, 62
fairness, 62, 130, 188
female directors, 174
fiduciary duty, 3, 66, 126, 128–129,
  133, 145, 152–153
fiduciary out, 126
financial distress costs, 84, 90, 97
financial flexibility, 98
financial instruments, 66
financial intermediaries, 64, 73
financial management, 1, 7, 33, 35,
  107, 134, 143, 145, 164, 198
financial markets, 4, 197
financial model, 33–34
financial modeling, 25
financial statements, 26
financial value, 9, 35
financing, 30
Friedman, Milton, 144

firm, 3
firm value, 17
fixed ratio, 115
floating ratio, 115
flow, 23, 26
Ford Motor Company, 147
foreign direct investment (FDI), 134
Foreign Investment Risk Review
  Modernization Act (FIRRMA), 135
forward triangle merger, 118
founder families, 172
founders, 182
framings, 153
free cash flow, 18, 22, 25, 31, 36, 41,
  43, 57, 84, 137
free cash flow hypothesis, 98–99
free ride, 189
Fujitsu, 135

G
G20/OECD corporate governance
  code, 167
gender equality, 197
General American Oil, 132
Generally Accepted Accounting
  Principles (GAAP), 158
G-index, 178
Glass Lewis, 174, 188
going concern, 22
golden parachute, 133, 178
Goldman, Sachs, 174
Google, 71, 109, 138
Gompers, Paul, 178
government intervention, 134
Government Pension Investment
  Fund (GPIF), 161
government, 134
Grab, 74
green-field investment, 36
greenhouse gas (GHG), 145, 156,
  159
greenshoe option, 69